Connecticut
Foundations of Reading
Practice Questions

DEAR FUTURE EXAM SUCCESS STORY

First of all, **THANK YOU** for purchasing Mometrix study materials!

Second, congratulations! You are one of the few determined test-takers who are committed to doing whatever it takes to excel on your exam. **You have come to the right place.** We developed these practice tests with one goal in mind: to deliver you the best possible approximation of the questions you will see on test day.

Standardized testing is one of the biggest obstacles on your road to success, which only increases the importance of doing well in the high-pressure, high-stakes environment of test day. Your results on this test could have a significant impact on your future, and these practice tests will give you the repetitions you need to build your familiarity and confidence with the test content and format to help you achieve your full potential on test day.

Your success is our success

We would love to hear from you! If you would like to share the story of your exam success or if you have any questions or comments in regard to our products, please contact us at **800-673-8175** or **support@mometrix.com**.

Thanks again for your business and we wish you continued success!

Sincerely,
The Mometrix Test Preparation Team

Copyright © 2023 by Mometrix Media LLC. All rights reserved.
Written and edited by the Mometrix Exam Secrets Test Prep Team
Printed in the United States of America

TABLE OF CONTENTS

Practice Test #1

Multiple Choice Questions

1. "Verbal dyspraxia" refers to:
- a. Trouble with the motor skills involved in speaking
- b. Confusing word or sentence order while speaking
- c. Misplacement of letters within words
- d. An inability to process verbal information

2. Which classroom instructional strategy would most likely assist ELLs with developing phonemic awareness skills?
- a. Practicing phonemic awareness skills on familiar vocabulary words in English
- b. Practicing phonemic awareness skills using only words in their native languages
- c. Introducing phonemes that are not part of their native languages first
- d. Teaching the English alphabet and alphabetic principle before teaching phonemic awareness skills

3. Which of the following examples best demonstrates a child who has not yet developed an understanding of book concepts?
- a. A first-grade student always looks to the pictures to figure out unknown words rather than using phonics strategies.
- b. A preschool student often holds books upside down and turns pages randomly.
- c. A kindergarten student inconsistently uses a return sweep and sometimes forgets where to go next after completing a line of text.
- d. A first-grade student sometimes points to one printed word for every two or three spoken words.

4. To teach students nonverbal communication skills, what have some teachers discovered through experience?
- a. Nonverbal communication should be taught to students in large portions.
- b. Nonverbal communication should be taught using appropriate situations.
- c. Nonverbal communication does not require students to have confidence.
- d. Nonverbal communication does not involve creativity from the students.

5. A kindergarten teacher asks students to say the word *cart*. She then tells students to take away the /t/ sound and tell her what they get. Which type of phonemic awareness activity are students practicing?
- a. Onset and rime manipulation
- b. Segmenting
- c. Phoneme isolation
- d. Phoneme deletion

1

Copyright © Mometrix Media. You have been licensed one copy of this document for personal use only. Any other reproduction or redistribution is strictly prohibited. All rights reserved. This content is provided for test preparation purposes only and does not imply an endorsement by Mometrix of any particular political, scientific, or religious point of view.

6. Alex is a first-grade student. His teacher notices that he commonly substitutes words that make sense in the sentences but don't match the print. For example, he recently said, "The car drove down a street," while the text actually said, "The car drove down the street." Which cueing system is Alex using?

    a. Graphophonic
    b. Semantic
    c. Syntactic
    d. Pragmatic

7. A first-grade teacher wants to help students compare and contrast short vowel sounds. Which activity would best assist students with this skill?

    a. Segmenting words with short vowel sounds using Elkonin boxes
    b. Tracing words with short vowel sounds using stencils
    c. Sorting words containing short vowel sounds
    d. Including words with short vowel sounds on the weekly spelling list

8. A first-grade student struggles to decode words containing *oo* in their spellings because that vowel combination makes two common sounds. Which prompt would be most likely to assist the student with decoding these words when encountered in texts?

    a. Look for parts of the word you already know.
    b. Use visual clues to guess the word and make sure that your guess looks right.
    c. Read the word both ways in the sentence to see which way makes sense.
    d. Think of similar words you know that have the same spelling pattern.

9. What is true about pre-production activities that teachers can use to encourage English-language speech by ELL students?

    a. Narrating students' actions will simply make them self-conscious.
    b. The activities that teachers use should involve hands-on learning.
    c. It is more important that activities use speech than have meaning.
    d. Language functions are irrelevant if students complete the lesson.

10. According to recent research findings, reading difficulties are primarily _____ in origin.

    a. Neurological and developmental
    b. Environmental and ecological
    c. Neurological and environmental
    d. Developmental and environmental

11. A preschool teacher is reading nursery rhymes to students, putting deliberate emphasis on the rhyming words. Which reading-related skill is she trying to develop in her students?

    a. Phonological awareness
    b. Phonemic awareness
    c. Alphabetic principle
    d. Phonics

Copyright © Mometrix Media. You have been licensed one copy of this document for personal use only. Any other reproduction or redistribution is strictly prohibited. All rights reserved.
This content is provided for test preparation purposes only and does not imply an endorsement by Mometrix of any particular political, scientific, or religious point of view.

12. In phonics instruction, what is accurate relative to phonological discrimination exercises?

 a. Children's invented spellings may omit consonants, but never vowels.
 b. Children can discriminate short vowels more easily than long vowels.
 c. Children can discriminate long vowels more easily than short vowels.
 d. Children must learn to discriminate long vowels before short vowels in words.

13. Government-funded research has found which of the following about phonics instruction?

 a. It is equally effective regardless of whether it is systematic and explicit or not.
 b. It is more effective for children of certain socioeconomic levels than for others.
 c. It is equally effective regardless of the age or grade levels when introduced.
 d. It is more effective when students can understand and apply their learning.

14. Students in a sixth-grade classroom are preparing to deliver a persuasive speech to school administrators requesting additional playground equipment. As part of their preparations, students are learning to adjust the formality of their spoken language to match specific situations. In small groups, they are role playing how they would make requests to friends, teachers, and administrators. They are comparing and contrasting the appropriate language to use in each situation. Which oral language component are students practicing?

 a. Morphology
 b. Semantics
 c. Syntax
 d. Pragmatics

15. Which of the following examples best describes explicit and systematic phonics instruction?

 a. A teacher observes a student as he reads a book independently. When the student struggles to decode a word with a certain spelling pattern, the teacher intervenes and provides a mini-lesson on the skill.
 b. A teacher assesses her students' phonics skills regularly and uses the assessment data to plan flexible, targeted, small-group instruction on specific sounds and blends.
 c. A teacher conducts frequent surveys to learn more about her students' interests. She uses the results to select books on these topics. She then identifies a few phonics skills that can be taught using the text in each book.
 d. A teacher reads a big book aloud to her students. She stops on a page and asks students if they notice any patterns in the words. Students identify words that start with the same letter, end with the same suffixes, and more. The teacher briefly explains each of their observations.

16. Mr. Clark is conducting a daily phonics lesson. Today, the class is focusing on the *st* consonant blend. Students first repeatedly produce the sound the blend makes. They then search for *st* words within the classroom. Which approach to phonics instruction is Mr. Clark demonstrating?

 a. Implicit
 b. Explicit
 c. Whole language
 d. Analytical

Copyright © Mometrix Media. You have been licensed one copy of this document for personal use only. Any other reproduction or redistribution is strictly prohibited. All rights reserved. This content is provided for test preparation purposes only and does not imply an endorsement by Mometrix of any particular political, scientific, or religious point of view.

17. A second-grade teacher is designing a word sort to help her students identify inflectional endings. Which pair of words should she use in this activity? *ed / ing*

    a. Jumped and eating
    b. *Blew* and *boo*
    c. Crunch and trash
    d. *Day* and *weigh*

18. A second-grade teacher is reading a student's journal entry and sees the following set of sentences:

> "I lisened to a great story. Then my teacher asked a question, and I ansered it."

Based on these sentences, which skill would be most beneficial for the teacher to focus on with the student?

    a. Consonant blends
    b. Consonant digraphs
    c. Silent letter spelling patterns
    d. Subject/verb agreement

19. A teacher initiates a guessing game to promote phonological awareness with first-graders. The teacher presents picture cards and speaks each word depicted very slowly (e.g., "sssssuuuuunnnnn") to emphasize its phonemes; children must guess the words. Which phonological process does this teach?

    a. Blending phonemes
    b. Deleting phonemes
    c. Segmenting phonemes
    d. Substituting phonemes

20. For an instructional activity to develop phonological awareness in K-1 students, which of these would teach them segmentation on multiple phonological levels?

    a. Teaching children how to separate sentences into the individual words that make up each sentence
    b. Teaching children to divide sentences into words, words into syllables, and syllables into phonemes
    c. Teaching children to divide words into individual syllables, or to divide words into onsets and rimes
    d. Teaching children how to separate short, monosyllabic words into individual component phonemes

21. How does environmental print contribute to reading development?

    a. It helps children apply the alphabetic principle.
    b. It often contains words that are easily decodable.
    c. It models one-to-one correspondence.
    d. It helps children understand that print contains meaning.

Copyright © Mometrix Media. You have been licensed one copy of this document for personal use only. Any other reproduction or redistribution is strictly prohibited. All rights reserved.
This content is provided for test preparation purposes only and does not imply an endorsement by Mometrix of any particular political, scientific, or religious point of view.

22. A fourth-grade student struggles to decode several words in her science textbook, including *organism*, *conclusion*, and *prediction*. Which strategy would best help the student decode these and other similar words?

    a. Using context clues to select words that make sense in the sentences
    b. Slowly stretching out the letter sounds
    c. Blending the phonemes
    d. Looking for known word parts, such as prefixes and suffixes   *Multisyllabic instruction*

23. In which of the following sentences would it be most appropriate to suggest that a first-grade student use the "sound it out" strategy to decode the underlined word?

    a. The child started to <u>tear</u> the wrapping paper off the gift.
    b. The <u>chain</u> on the swing was squeaky. *Chain*
    c. The kitten was hiding behind the <u>curtain</u>.
    d. The dolphin swam across the <u>ocean</u>.

24. While reading a book about animals, a student struggles to decode the word *giraffe*. He then points to the picture and says, "Those are giraffes. I saw them at the zoo." Which cueing system is the student using to figure out the unknown word?

    a. Semantic
    b. Syntactic
    c. Graphophonic
    d. Pragmatic

25. Ms. Peterson is reading a big book to her kindergarten students. She shows them where the title and author's name are located on the cover. She then tracks the text with her finger as she reads. What is Ms. Peterson modeling for her students?

    a. Concepts of print
    b. Phonological awareness
    c. Phonemic awareness
    d. Close reading

26. A group of students is playing a card game at a classroom reading center. They take turns flipping over two cards and trying to create matches. Each match consists of a letter and a picture of a word that begins with that letter. For example, a student matches a card containing a letter *p* and a card displaying a picture of a pig. What concept are students practicing?

    a. Encoding
    b. One-to-one correspondence
    c. Phoneme isolation
    d. Alphabetic principle

27. A second-grade reading teacher notices that her students are decoding words accurately but struggle with appropriate phrasing and expression. Which activity would most likely help her students improve in this area?

    a. Introducing new texts of varied genres for students to read aloud independently
    b. Listening to audio versions of texts
    c. Leading students in repeated choral readings of familiar texts
    d. Participating in partner-reading experiences

Copyright © Mometrix Media. You have been licensed one copy of this document for personal use only. Any other reproduction or redistribution is strictly prohibited. All rights reserved. This content is provided for test preparation purposes only and does not imply an endorsement by Mometrix of any particular political, scientific, or religious point of view.

28. Laura is reading an expository text and struggles to decode the words *rabbit* and *problem*. Which spelling pattern would be most beneficial for the teacher to practice with Laura?

    a. Open syllables
    b. Closed syllables
    c. CVCC spelling patterns
    d. Double consonants

29. Which of the following examples best demonstrates an intensive intervention plan for a student whose assessment results show she is performing below benchmark levels in decoding consonant blends?

    a. Sending home leveled readers containing numerous consonant blends for the student to read with family members
    b. Requiring the student to complete independent activities related to consonant blends during the daily word work station
    c. Adding 15 minutes of small-group instruction on consonant blends four times per week
    d. Teaching a whole-class lesson on consonant blends, followed by multiple independent practice activities

30. "Code knowledge" facilitates reading fluency because:

    a. It brings the entirety of the student's previous experience to bear on decoding a text.
    b. It offers a framework for organizing new information by assigning code words to sets of ideas.
    c. There is no such thing as "code knowledge." The correct term is "core knowledge."
    d. It offers a systematic approach to untangling the wide variety of vowel sounds when an unfamiliar word is encountered.

31. Among some of the critical components of good phonics lessons, which one is taught for the purpose of helping students to decode unfamiliar words?

    a. Introducing sound-spellings
    b. Blending phonemes into words
    c. Discriminating phonemes in words
    d. Reviewing to overlearn sound-spellings

32. Researchers have found which of these about instruction in phonological awareness?

    a. All children benefit highly from receiving instruction in phonological awareness.
    b. Children at risk for speech or language delays benefit the most from this teaching.
    c. Some children benefit little from this instruction, and some do not benefit at all.
    d. This instruction only benefits children who have normal language development.

33. Which type of blending of phonemes into words is the best technique for diagnostically pinpointing individual student problem areas in phonics instruction?

    a. Successive blending
    b. Silent blending
    c. Final blending
    d. Line blending

Copyright © Mometrix Media. You have been licensed one copy of this document for personal use only. Any other reproduction or redistribution is strictly prohibited. All rights reserved. This content is provided for test preparation purposes only and does not imply an endorsement by Mometrix of any particular political, scientific, or religious point of view.

34. Which of the following spelling patterns is usually taught to children first?

a. CVCe
b. CVVC
c. CVC
d. CCVC

[handwritten: ✱ CVC spelling patterns taught to children first.]

35. On a continuum, which of these represents the most complex level of phonological awareness?

a. Segmenting words into their individual syllables and blending individual syllables into words
b. Phonemic awareness, i.e., understanding words consist of phonemes and manipulating these
c. Segmenting words into their onsets and rimes and blending onsets and rimes into full words
d. Segmenting sentences, i.e., understanding speech consists of separate words; rhyming songs

36. Among the three cueing systems, which of the following aspects of reading comprehension belongs in the category of the semantic cueing system?

a. Grammar
b. Word order
c. Word meaning
d. Sentence structure

37. Regarding the relationship of phonemic awareness to reading and writing, which is NOT true?

a. Phonemic awareness is a listening and speaking skill, not a reading and writing skill.
b. Including print letters and words in teaching phonemic awareness is more effective.
c. Using print letters and words alone in teaching phonemic awareness is sufficient.
d. Pointing to printed letters while saying them aloud to draw attention to sound-letter connections is helpful.

38. Regarding student problems that teachers may observe which can indicate dyslexia, which is true?

a. Dyslexic students perform worse on objective tests than their IQ and knowledge.
b. Students with dyslexia typically have more trouble reading long than short words.
c. Students who have dyslexia lack fluidity, but fare much better with rote memory.
d. Dyslexic students have equal trouble understanding words in isolation or context.

39. In learning the alphabetic principle, which do children typically develop first?

a. They learn the shapes of letters.
b. They learn the sounds of letters.
c. They learn these all concurrently.
d. They learn the names of letters.

Copyright © Mometrix Media. You have been licensed one copy of this document for personal use only. Any other reproduction or redistribution is strictly prohibited. All rights reserved.
This content is provided for test preparation purposes only and does not imply an endorsement by Mometrix of any particular political, scientific, or religious point of view.

40. According to the Center on Instruction (COI), which of the choices below accurately describes one of several recommendations for teaching adolescent literacy?

    a. Teach effective use of comprehension strategies only in discrete lessons.

    b. Set high standards for text and vocabulary, not questions or conversation.

    c. Focus on student engagement during reading more than motivation to read.

    d. Instruct necessary content knowledge for students' crucial concept mastery.

41. The teacher provides students with a more advanced passage of reading, in which there are a variety of new words that many of the students do not know how to pronounce. How might the teacher go about helping the students in pronouncing the new words?

    a. Hint at the correct pronunciation with a variety of different rhyming words

    b. Assist the students in sounding out the words phonetically, by recognizing rules for vowels and consonants

    c. Have the students look up the words in a dictionary to review the pronunciation information that is provided there

    d. Ask students who are already familiar with the words to a help their classmates in pronouncing the new words

42. Early in the school year, all members of a group of kindergarten students are able to chant the alphabet. The teacher is now teaching the students what the alphabet looks like in written form. The teacher points to a letter, and the students vocalize the corresponding sound. Alternatively, the teacher vocalizes a phoneme and a student points to it on the alphabet chart. The teacher is using _____ in her instruction.

    a. letter–sound correspondence

    b. rote memorization

    c. predictive analysis

    d. segmentation

43. Regarding these elements of print awareness in literacy development, which is true?

    a. All students with normal development can differentiate printed words from spaces.

    b. To identify initial and final letters in words, students must identify words vs. spaces.

    c. The only students not automatically knowing left-right directionality are certain ELLs.

    d. Being able to identify basic punctuation is not important to reading comprehension.

44. Children develop phonological awareness:

    a. Only through direct training given by adults

    b. Only naturally, through exposure to language

    c. Via both natural exposure and direct training

    d. Via neither incidental exposure nor instruction

45. Which element of the process approach to writing is most related to metacognition?

    a. Self-evaluation

    b. Student interactions

    c. Authentic audiences

    d. Personal responsibility

Copyright © Mometrix Media. You have been licensed one copy of this document for personal use only. Any other reproduction or redistribution is strictly prohibited. All rights reserved. This content is provided for test preparation purposes only and does not imply an endorsement by Mometrix of any particular political, scientific, or religious point of view.

46. Of the following examples, which one is NOT an open-ended question?

    a. "When does the climax of this story occur?"
    b. "Is this expression a simile or a metaphor?"
    c. "How are similes and metaphors different?"
    d. "What are some reasons we have poetry?"

47. Cognates and realia are most useful for teaching which component of reading instruction to ELLs?

    a. Vocabulary
    b. Prosody
    c. Phonological awareness
    d. Phonemic awareness

48. Which of the following questions is focused on students' aesthetic responses to a text?

    a. Which character is the protagonist in the story?
    b. What is the conflict in the story?
    c. How did you feel when the character was being treated poorly by her friends?
    d. What genre does this story fit into?

49. Based on assessment data, a teacher identifies a small group of students who would benefit from targeted instruction on using textual evidence to support their answers. Which strategy would be most helpful for the teacher to model to assist students with this type of test question?

    a. Underlining passages in the text where answers are located
    b. Reading the passage once to identify the main idea, and then rereading to look for details
    c. Reading each answer choice carefully before selecting an answer, crossing out answers as they are eliminated
    d. Completing a story map while reading the story

50. An ELL is having difficulties comprehending a science textbook because it contains many unknown vocabulary words with few accompanying visuals. Which instructional strategy would most likely assist the student with this difficulty?

    a. Reading the textbook aloud to him rather than asking him to read it independently
    b. Supplying him with an audio version of the textbook
    c. Providing him with a printed outline of each chapter's main points
    d. Giving him access to a multimedia version of the textbook to view on his computer

51. The use of which graphic organizer best supports schema theory?

    a. Problem-solution chart
    b. Think-pair-share chart
    c. Sequence chain
    d. KWL chart

Copyright © Mometrix Media. You have been licensed one copy of this document for personal use only. Any other reproduction or redistribution is strictly prohibited. All rights reserved.
This content is provided for test preparation purposes only and does not imply an endorsement by Mometrix of any particular political, scientific, or religious point of view.

52. A second grader is reading a page from a narrative text. Halfway through the page, he stops and says, "Wait! This doesn't make sense. I think I read something wrong." What type of skill is the student demonstrating?

    a. Decoding skills
    b. Metacognitive skills
    c. Evaluative skills
    d. Application skills

53. To help students understand abstract concepts in the print materials they read, which instructional aids that teachers provide can students always use three-dimensionally?

    a. Examples
    b. Manipulatives
    c. Graphic organizers
    d. Charts, tables, graphs

54. A teacher gives students the following set of words: *compare, organism, predict, cell, habitat,* and *conclude.* Students are instructed to sort the words into two categories. What is the primary purpose of this activity?

    a. Classifying words according to morphology
    b. Recognizing common spelling patterns used to decode words
    c. Differentiating between academic and content vocabulary
    d. Grouping words with similar meanings

55. Which strategy can be used to build readers' confidence and increase both comprehension and fluency when introducing an unknown text?

    a. Introducing new vocabulary before reading
    b. Reading the first few pages aloud before asking students to finish it independently
    c. Listing what students want to learn about the topic
    d. Asking students to predict what the text will be about based on the title and cover

56. Students in a fourth-grade class are reading and analyzing a fictional book about a girl, Samantha, who finds a wallet in the parking lot of a store. Which student response best demonstrates a prediction made using text evidence?

    a. I think the book is mostly about honesty because Samantha ultimately decided to return the money she found.
    b. I think Samantha will return the money because that is what I would do in her situation.
    c. I think the author wrote the book to teach readers about the importance of being honest.
    d. I think Samantha will decide to return the money because this chapter ends with her thinking about the bills the owner may need to pay with the money inside.

57. Among practices for differentiating reading instruction, which of these represents a valid one?

    a. Materials used for read-alouds should be for fun and not common teaching texts.
    b. Teachers should instruct the whole class uniformly by using the same single text.
    c. Teachers should reserve enough class time for students to read at comfort levels.
    d. To reach all student reading levels, teachers should base each unit upon the text.

Copyright © Mometrix Media. You have been licensed one copy of this document for personal use only. Any other reproduction or redistribution is strictly prohibited. All rights reserved. This content is provided for test preparation purposes only and does not imply an endorsement by Mometrix of any particular political, scientific, or religious point of view.

58. In which of the following mechanical writing conventions should teachers instruct typically developing students in grades K-2?

    a. Capitalizing salutations and closings in letters
    b. Capitalizing the initial word of each sentence
    c. Capitalizing names of months and weekdays
    d. Capitalizing names of holidays and countries

59. Which of the following options would be the most effective way to modify a cloze reading passage for struggling readers to assist them with completing the task while still allowing them to practice the skill?

    a. Providing the first few letters of each answer
    b. Including a word bank
    c. Having students work in pairs
    d. Including no more than three omitted words

60. Fourth-grade students in Mr. Lee's class are writing persuasive speeches on topics of their choice and presenting them to the class. One student, Caleb, gives a speech regarding the types of foods the school cafeteria should serve. He states, "The cafeteria should stop serving meatloaf because nobody likes it." After the speech, Mr. Lee asks Caleb what research he conducted to arrive at that conclusion. Caleb responds by saying, "Nobody at my lunch table ever eats it. They just end up throwing it away at the end of lunch." Which type of faulty reasoning should Mr. Lee address with Caleb?

    a. Illogical conclusion
    b. Overgeneralization   *Overgeneralization*
    c. Personal bias
    d. Circular reasoning

61. While reading an expository text aloud to students, a teacher makes the following comments.

> "'The cheetah can accelerate to its top speed in about three seconds.' Hmm, I'm not sure what accelerate means. Let me read that again to see if the sentence has any clues. 'The cheetah can accelerate to its top speed in about three seconds.' It has something to do with the cheetah getting faster, so I think accelerate means to speed up."

What is the teacher demonstrating in this activity?

    a. Forming mental images   *Thinking aloud*
    b. Making a prediction
    c. Thinking aloud
    d. Visualizing

Copyright © Mometrix Media. You have been licensed one copy of this document for personal use only. Any other reproduction or redistribution is strictly prohibited. All rights reserved.
This content is provided for test preparation purposes only and does not imply an endorsement by Mometrix of any particular political, scientific, or religious point of view.

62. Students in Ms. Dean's class discuss their existing knowledge and thoughts about sustainable farming practices before conducting any research on the topic. Next, they research the topic, locating four reputable print sources and conducting one interview with an expert in the field. They take notes, recording key information from each source. They use their notes from all of the sources to write a research report on the topic. They also complete a written reflection outlining how their initial thoughts have changed as a result of the new information gathered from the sources. Which comprehension strategy are students demonstrating?

    a. Evaluating
    b. Inferring
    c. Drawing conclusions
    d. Synthesizing   *Synthesizing*

63. Of the following influences on student reading comprehension, which one is a psychological factor?   *Motivation*

    a. Attention
    b. Perception
    c. Motivation
    d. Working memory

64. Regarding the reading strategy of summarizing text, which of the following is most accurate about what will help students support their reading comprehension?

    a. It will help them to identify important ideas, but not to organize them.
    b. It will help them to identify themes, problems, and solutions in a text.
    c. It will help them to monitor comprehension more than to sequence it.
    d. It will help them to make visual the connections with text they realize.

65. A sixth-grade student is struggling to comprehend several different types of nonfiction texts. Which strategy would be most likely to assist him with this difficulty?

    a. Asking him to reread the text multiple times to locate key information
    b. Providing him with a story map to complete while reading
    c. Teaching him to recognize the features of different nonfiction text structures
    d. Asking him to summarize the main points of each text

66. A fifth-grade teacher is helping his students analyze how varied sentence structure contributes to the tone and mood of a text. Which of the following sentences should he use if he wants to model a complex sentence?

    a. Michael ate pancakes for breakfast.
    b. Michael ate breakfast and brushed his teeth.
    c. Before going to school, Michael brushed his teeth.
    d. Michael ate breakfast, and he brushed his teeth.

Copyright © Mometrix Media. You have been licensed one copy of this document for personal use only. Any other reproduction or redistribution is strictly prohibited. All rights reserved. This content is provided for test preparation purposes only and does not imply an endorsement by Mometrix of any particular political, scientific, or religious point of view.

67. Which of these is accurate about instruction that supports independent, reflective student reading?

 a. Students typically write in reader response journals after both sustained silent and independent reading.
 b. Student journals enable teachers to monitor reading, check comprehension, discuss, and suggest books.
 c. Students typically can write in reader response journals without any modeling, prompting, or references.
 d. Students should be advised to achieve a balance of 50 percent reading and 50 percent writing.

68. A teacher explains and models steps for fourth-grade students to follow in asking and answering research questions using text and text features. Which represents the most effective sequence for these steps?

 a. Write research questions, use table of contents and headings in selected text to find information, read identified chapters for pertinent information, classify or categorize information by which question it answers
 b. Use table of contents and headings in selected text to find information, read identified chapters for pertinent information, classify or categorize information by which question it answers, write research questions
 c. Read identified chapters for pertinent information, write research questions, classify or categorize information by which question it answers, use table of contents and headings in selected text to find information
 d. Classify or categorize information by which question it answers, use table of contents and headings in selected text to find information, write research questions, read identified chapters for pertinent information

69. Explicit instruction in reading comprehension strategies is found more effective in research. Which component of explicit instruction is reflected when a teacher reads text the students are reading while conducting a "think-aloud?"

 a. Modeling
 b. Application
 c. Guided practice
 d. Direct explanation

70. In an unfamiliar word encountered while reading, a student does not recognize the first part of the word, but does recognize that it ends in *-tion,* meaning it is a noun and the first part probably derives from a verb. Which term best describes the syllable *-tion*?

 a. A phoneme
 b. A morpheme
 c. A grapheme
 d. A sememe

Copyright © Mometrix Media. You have been licensed one copy of this document for personal use only. Any other reproduction or redistribution is strictly prohibited. All rights reserved. This content is provided for test preparation purposes only and does not imply an endorsement by Mometrix of any particular political, scientific, or religious point of view.

71. A teacher wants to work on her students' listening comprehension in addition to their reading comprehension since she understands that the skills are interrelated. She has a series of short stories that she thinks the students will enjoy. Which of the following would be the best supplement to typical written comprehension exercises?

    a. Preview the content and then read the stories aloud to the students. Assess listening comprehension through verbal and written questions.

    b. Ask the students to choose one story each to read aloud to a small group. Encourage the students to discuss what they have learned afterward.

    c. Assign each student a story to read and require them to write a report on it. Each student should then present his or her report based on what he or she has learned to the class.

    d. Have the students read stories aloud to the class, and create mock tests based upon the main ideas which they identify.

72. A third-grade teacher decides to introduce new vocabulary words using a word association game. What is required in order for the students to succeed with word associations?

    a. The definition of the new words

    b. Prior knowledge

    c. The spelling of the word

    d. Synonyms of the new words

73. Which of the following genres is most important for children just beginning to become readers in grades K, 1, and 2?

    a. Alphabet books, wordless picture books, and easy-to-read books

    b. Legends and tall tales

    c. Biographies and informational books

    d. Chapter books and fantasy books

74. Which of the following reading comprehension strategies is *most* applicable to differentiating between homonyms without knowing their exact spellings?

    a. Pictures

    b. Phonics

    c. Context

    d. Grammar

75. An eighth-grade student is able to decode most words fluently and has a borderline/acceptable vocabulary, but his reading comprehension is quite low. He can be helped with instructional focus on:

    a. Strategies to increase comprehension and to build vocabulary

    b. Strategies to increase comprehension and to be able to identify correct syntactical usage

    c. Strategies to improve his understanding of both content and context

    d. Strategies to build vocabulary and to improve his understanding of both content and context

Copyright © Mometrix Media. You have been licensed one copy of this document for personal use only. Any other reproduction or redistribution is strictly prohibited. All rights reserved. This content is provided for test preparation purposes only and does not imply an endorsement by Mometrix of any particular political, scientific, or religious point of view.

76. A teacher notices that her new student, Carl, has a hard time answering questions related to comprehension during class and has scored low on comprehension quizzes and worksheets. What would be the most logical first step in determining how to help Carl?

a. Encourage Carl to read all assigned texts at least twice before class to help him understand what he has read.
b. Provide Carl with story maps of what he will be reading to assist his comprehension visually.
c. Ask Carl to read aloud with his teacher individually so that she can ensure that he is reading with expected accuracy and speed (i.e., fluently).
d. Modify Carl's class work so that he is able to work on easier comprehension material until his skills are brought up to speed.

77. Which of these is a strategy most applicable to evaluating a young student's reading comprehension of narrative writing?

a. Whether the student can retell a story that s/he has just read
b. Whether the student can decode unfamiliar words in the story
c. Whether the student can invent spellings for unfamiliar words
d. Whether the student can identify and produce rhyming words

78. Which instructional activity is the best example of the research-based strategy of activating students' prior knowledge before reading?

a. Before students read a text, the teacher instructs them in relevant background information.
b. Before and after they read a text, the teacher has students make a KWL chart on its subject.
c. After students have read a text, the teacher asks them what they know about the subject.
d. The teacher asks students to express their opinions and reactions on a topic after reading.

79. As an assessment, a teacher gives a student a cloze procedure. Which response is an example of a student reading strategy based primarily on using syntactic cues to meaning?

a. The missing word must be an adverb because the word it has to modify is the verb.
b. The missing word must be a bad thing, because the word describing it is "horrible."
c. The missing word must be an adjective because it is before the word that is a noun.
d. The missing word must be impossible to guess, because I read one word at a time.

80. What is one limitation of informal reading assessments?

a. They must be administered in a standardized fashion, increasing student anxiety.
b. The results may be subjective.
c. They require more time to plan and implement than formal assessments.
d. They are often costly to administer and score.

81. What is one benefit of using a rubric over other types of assessment techniques?

a. Rubrics break down overall scores by criteria, allowing students to see their strengths and weaknesses.
b. Rubrics allow students to track their progress over time.
c. Rubrics help students see how they did in comparison with their peers.
d. Rubrics help identify the types of reading miscues students are making so teachers can provide targeted instruction.

Copyright © Mometrix Media. You have been licensed one copy of this document for personal use only. Any other reproduction or redistribution is strictly prohibited. All rights reserved. This content is provided for test preparation purposes only and does not imply an endorsement by Mometrix of any particular political, scientific, or religious point of view.

82. When assessing oral reading fluency, which characteristic indicates a non-fluent reader?
  a. Simultaneous word identification and comprehension
  b. Automaticity and speed irrespective of expressiveness
  c. Perceiving chunks of information, not individual words
  d. Demonstrating an absence of effort with reading aloud

83. Which of the following is a way of determining that a reading assessment instrument is valid?
  a. The test items minimize guesswork by students.
  b. The test items measure the indicated construct.
  d. The test items are sufficiently large in numbers.
  d. The test items give consistent scores over time.

84. According to principles of educational measurement as applied to reading assessment, what is the most logical sequence for the following practices?
  a. Develop assessments, design curricula, adopt standards, set goals
  b. Set goals, adopt standards, design curricula, develop assessments
  c. Adopt standards, set goals, develop assessments, design curricula
  d. Design curricula, adopt standards, set goals, develop assessments

85. Among the following, which is an indicator of reliability in a reading assessment instrument?
  a. The test measures the reading skill it specifically claims to measure.
  b. The test measures the reading skill through open-ended questions.
  c. The test measures the reading skill using a few very focused items.
  d. The test measures the reading skill consistently over repeated uses.

86. To inform instructional strategies for writing mechanics, which of the following is an appropriate benchmark for students in grades 3-5?
  a. Using periods after declarative sentences
  b. Using question marks after interrogatives
  c. Using commas to divide a series of words
  d. Using quotation marks around quotations

87. Which of the following statements is typically true of literature circles?
  a. All students within a classroom read and discuss the same book.
  b. Teachers predetermine the questions and concepts that will be discussed.
  c. Students have choices about the books they read.
  d. Groups remain static throughout the year.

88. According to typical state and district English language proficiency (ELP) standards in comprehending oral communications, active listening for learning by third-grade ELL students includes understanding and following directions related to physical movement in space. These differ by level in which respect(s)?
  a. The number of steps a student can follow increases by level.
  b. The number of dimensions of movement increases by level.
  c. The numbers of both of these increase with ascending level.
  d. The numbers of neither of these increase according to level.

Copyright © Mometrix Media. You have been licensed one copy of this document for personal use only. Any other reproduction or redistribution is strictly prohibited. All rights reserved.
This content is provided for test preparation purposes only and does not imply an endorsement by Mometrix of any particular political, scientific, or religious point of view.

89. Which is least effective about instructing students in basic literary analysis skills, which (based on research results) are arranged in a hierarchy of progressive difficulty?

    a. Teachers should instruct one skill at a time to master before moving higher within the hierarchy.

    b. Teachers should address every skill in the hierarchy without waiting for students to master them.

    c. Teachers should frequently re-teach all skills all year using progressively more complex materials.

    d. Teachers should frequently evaluate students' skills throughout the year.

90. Which of the following is the best example of multimedia instructional materials to support reading?

    a. Books that incorporate many illustrations

    b. "Books on Tape" reading aloud recording

    c. Following in text as teacher reads it aloud

    d. Interactive, audiovisual, touchscreen text

91. A seventh grader has never had much success with reading. Her ability to decode is rudimentary; she stops and starts when reading, frequently loses her place, or misreads an important word. She doesn't seem aware of where errors occur, or she does not attempt to correct them. When asked about what she's read, her comprehension is minimal. To help her, instructional focus on which of the following would be most useful?

    a. Carefully organized lessons in decoding, sight words, vocabulary, and comprehension at least three to five times a week. These mini-lessons must be extremely clear, with the parts broken down to the lowest common denominator. The more tightly interwoven and systematized the instruction, the better chance this student will have.

    b. A weekly lesson focusing on one aspect of reading. This student will be overwhelmed if too many strategies are offered at once. The instruction should focus first on recognizing sight words, then letter–sound association. Next, the girl needs an understanding of the rules of syntax.

    c. The student isn't trying. Her instruction should be aimed at helping her learn to be self-motivated and disciplined in her approach to learning.

    d. Comprehension strategies will help her grasp the overall meaning of a text. From there she can begin to drill down until she's able to combine various approaches that, working together, will enable her to read.

92. When teachers assign students to take research notes on sources they find and read, what do they also need to advise students to do?

    a. To make more generalized notes rather than more detailed notes

    b. To note both quotations and paraphrases without differentiating

    c. To differentiate quoting, paraphrasing, and commentaries clearly

    d. To note both their own paraphrases and commentaries the same

93. Using small-group instruction enables teachers to do which of these?

    a. Teach main ideas or strategic integration

    b. Instruction in rhyming and onsets

    c. Use read-alouds for oral practice

    d. Diagnose reading difficulties and design reading interventions

Copyright © Mometrix Media. You have been licensed one copy of this document for personal use only. Any other reproduction or redistribution is strictly prohibited. All rights reserved.
This content is provided for test preparation purposes only and does not imply an endorsement by Mometrix of any particular political, scientific, or religious point of view.

94. A teacher has challenged a student with a book about Antarctica that is just beyond the high end of the student's Instructional level. The teacher points out that the student already knows quite a bit about penguins because the class studied them earlier in the year. He reminds the student that she's recently seen a television show about the seals that also live in Antarctic waters. The teacher gives the student a list of words she's likely to find in the text, and they discuss what those words might mean. The student begins to read, but stops to ask the teacher what *circumpolar* means. The teacher is also unfamiliar with the word, but reminds her that *circum* is a prefix. The student recalls that it means "about or around" and deduces that circumpolar most likely refers to something found around or in a polar region. This instructional approach is called:

    a. Modular instruction
    b. Scaffolding
    c. Linking
    d. Transmutation

95. Prekindergarten students tell their teacher, Mr. Clark, that they want to write about their field trip to the zoo. Mr. Clark writes down the students' sentences on chart paper, and then reads them back to the class, pointing to each word and modeling appropriate fluency. After reading the story multiple times, Mr. Clark invites the students to read with him. Which type of interaction is Mr. Clark demonstrating?

    a. Language experience approach
    b. Writing workshop
    c. Trait-based writing
    d. Modeled writing

96. In the gradual release model of individual and group reading lessons, which represents the correct sequence of activities?

    a. Modeling and demonstration, teacher-led collaboration, guided practice, student-led collaboration, independent practice
    b. Guided practice, independent practice, teacher-led collaboration, student-led collaboration, modeling and demonstration
    c. Teacher-led collaboration, student-led collaboration, modeling and demonstration, guided practice, independent practice
    d. Independent practice, guided practice, student-led collaboration, teacher-led collaboration, modeling and demonstration

97. A teacher plans to use a rubric to define learning objectives for a class instructional unit, guide students in completing their assignments, and serve as a unit assessment. Which statement is most applicable to incorporating student input into assessment design?

    a. So many premade rubrics are available online, it is unnecessary to "reinvent the wheel."
    b. Only the teacher, who knows learning objectives and how to do it, should create a rubric.
    c. The teacher should collect student input on objectives and assignments to create a rubric.
    d. The students and teacher should all work together in designing the rubric collaboratively.

Copyright © Mometrix Media. You have been licensed one copy of this document for personal use only. Any other reproduction or redistribution is strictly prohibited. All rights reserved. This content is provided for test preparation purposes only and does not imply an endorsement by Mometrix of any particular political, scientific, or religious point of view.

98. Arthur writes a paper. One classmate identifies ideas and words that resonated with her when she read it. Another describes how reading the paper changed his thinking. A third asks Arthur some questions about what he meant by certain statements in the paper. A fourth suggests a portion of the paper that needs more supporting information. This description is most typical of which of the following?

    a. Portfolio assessment
    b. Holistic scoring
    c. Scoring rubric
    d. Peer review

99. Which of the following teacher actions would most effectively encourage reading development in students' home environments?

    a. Reminding students to read with their parents each day
    b. Sending home a weekly update listing the phonics skills the class practiced
    c. Sending home a list of weekly spelling words for students to memorize
    d. Sending home leveled texts for students to read with family members

100. Which choice is the best method of structuring language arts curriculum and instruction?

    a. Examine all state-level or national standardized tests that students will be required to take. Structure the curriculum and lessons to address all concepts included in the tests, with an attempt to proportion the time spent in a way that mirrors the breakdown of the tests.
    b. Research the instructional methods used in supplemental education fields. Use those newer methods of introducing and reinforcing concepts in class to ensure that students are receiving consistent and standard instruction.
    c. Use the written curriculum provided by the school district or specific campus as a foundation for instruction. Schedule regular planning sessions to incorporate a variety of texts and instruction methods, as well as to coordinate instruction with teachers of other subjects.
    d. Plan sequential units of study that focus on isolated skills such as word and vocabulary study, comprehension strategies, listening, viewing, and speaking. Design lessons to focus on the mastery of one skill at a time with the goal of studying the relationship between skills toward the end of the school year.

Integration of Knowledge and Understanding

101. Using the information from the following exhibits and your pedagogical knowledge related to literacy and English language arts, write a response of approximately 400-600 words in which you:

- Discuss one strength and one area for improvement exhibited by the student related to language and literacy development
- Identify one instructional strategy, approach, or activity that could be applied to support the student's strengths and learning needs
- Explain why the instructional strategy, approach, or activity you identified would be appropriate and effective for this purpose
- Support your reasoning with specific examples from the exhibits and your pedagogical knowledge and skills related to English language arts and literacy development

Be sure to support your response with specific examples from all three exhibits.

Copyright © Mometrix Media. You have been licensed one copy of this document for personal use only. Any other reproduction or redistribution is strictly prohibited. All rights reserved.
This content is provided for test preparation purposes only and does not imply an endorsement by Mometrix of any particular political, scientific, or religious point of view.

EXHIBIT 1

TEACHER NOTES

Student: Madelynn **Age:** 7 **Grade:** 2

Home Language: English **IEP?:** No

10/1: I met Madelynn's mom at open-house last night and she gave me some insight into Madelynn's interests. She said that getting Madelynn to read at home is a struggle because she often becomes frustrated and bored. Her mother did say that Madelynn sometimes enjoys reading nonfiction books, particularly about animals.

10/4: Today I conducted oral reading fluency screenings for fall. Madelynn's rate is 40 WCPM, which is eleven less than the fall 50th percentile benchmark of 51 WCPM with an accuracy rate of 90%. She seemed unfocused and tried to read as quickly as possible without paying much attention to accuracy. Several times, she trailed off and began to mumble as she read, and it became difficult to understand her. She demonstrated significant gaps in overall comprehension and had difficulty pronouncing some multisyllabic words.

10/6: Today students gave oral presentations on self-selected reading books. Madelynn chose a nonfiction book about reptiles and gave a fantastic presentation. She recalled several details about reptiles and explained key facts about them very well. Madelynn was clearly interested in the topic. This presentation went much better than her last one after reading an assigned fictional book.

10/10: To introduce a social studies unit on landforms, students independently read an informational passage and completed corresponding activities. The passage was lengthier than the class was used to, and although Madelynn typically prefers nonfiction, she appeared visibly overwhelmed and frustrated. Several times, I noticed her staring off into the distance and had to redirect her attention. She did not complete the reading assignment in the twenty minutes allotted.

EXHIBIT 2

READING LITERATURE

The teacher administers an oral reading assessment and records their performance to determine their oral reading fluency. After having them read aloud a grade-level passage, the teacher asks corresponding comprehension questions. Madelynn's performance record is shown below, followed by a transcript of the conversation between Madelynn and the teacher about the text.

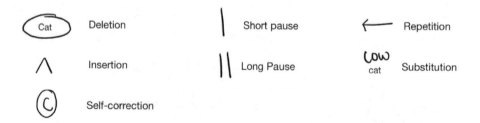

Copyright © Mometrix Media. You have been licensed one copy of this document for personal use only. Any other reproduction or redistribution is strictly prohibited. All rights reserved.
This content is provided for test preparation purposes only and does not imply an endorsement by Mometrix of any particular political, scientific, or religious point of view.

READING PASSAGE

Title: The Magic Fairy Garden

"I think it just needs a few more sparkly rocks." Amelia thought to herself as she put the finishing touches on her ~finished~ new fairy garden. *feather ©*

"There we go! It's beautiful!" she exclaimed. For days, Amelia had been carefully planning the details and gathering materials to create the most perfect fairy garden that anyone had ever seen. She used cardboard to *getting mats crate* make benches, built a gate with craft sticks, and decorated it with fresh cut flowers, sticks, leaves, and the most *beaches* *stacks leafs* sparkly rocks that she could find in her backyard. *yard*

"This is sure to bring out all of the fairies!" Amelia said to herself. "I can't wait to see them all!"

That night, Amelia waited and waited by her bedroom window hoping to catch a glimpse of a magical fairy, but *hopping© the©* nothing seemed to be happening. Amelia began to grow tired. Her eyes were heavy and she started to yawn. *was get*

"Why don't the fairies want to come and see my beautiful garden? I worked so hard on it!" she said *work* disappointedly. After what seemed like hours of waiting and watching, Amelia finally drifted off to sleep. *how waiting dried*

Suddenly, Amelia was startled awake by a strange, mysterious rustling sound outside. She slowly peeled off her *strong* *peered* blankets and quietly tiptoed over to her window. When she pulled back the curtain, you would not believe what *of* she saw! A tiny green speck of light was dancing around her fairy garden! Just as soon as it appeared, it flew away *the* into the night.

"Could that have been a fairy?", Amelia wondered. *wander*

After Madelynn reads the passage aloud, the teacher asks some comprehension questions to determine her level of understanding about what he has read. Below is a transcript of their conversation.

Teacher: What was the title of this story?

Madelynn: I can't remember the whole thing. The....something about a garden I think.

Copyright © Mometrix Media. You have been licensed one copy of this document for personal use only. Any other reproduction or redistribution is strictly prohibited. All rights reserved.
This content is provided for test preparation purposes only and does not imply an endorsement by Mometrix of any particular political, scientific, or religious point of view.

Teacher: Do you think this story was fiction or nonfiction?

Madelynn: It's probably made-up.

Teacher: Who was the main character of this story?

Madelynn: A little girl named Emily...I mean...Amy. No, Amelia!

Teacher: Good! What was Amelia doing in the story?

Madelynn: Making a garden.

Teacher: Where did the story take place?

Madelynn: Probably outside.

Teacher: What makes you think so?

Madelynn: Because that's where people usually make gardens.

Teacher: Do you remember what kind of garden she was making?

Madelynn: One that she made with a bunch of different stuff.

Teacher: Who did she want to come visit the garden?

Madelynn: Let me think...(*long pause*)...oh yeah! Fairies, right?

Teacher: Yes! Did they visit her?

Madelynn: Yep!

Teacher: What sort of items did Amelia put in her garden?

Madelynn: I can't really remember that. Maybe she planted some seeds. Or a tree. I would probably want to plant seeds in a garden.

Teacher: What was the problem Amelia had in the story?

Madelynn: It took a long time to decorate. And then she fell asleep.

Teacher: Do you remember how the story ended?

Madelynn: I only just remember that she was sleeping.

EXHIBIT 3
READING INFORMATIONAL TEXT

After a slide show presentation on various landforms, the teacher gives each student an informational reading along with a matching activity and corresponding comprehension questions for students to answer in their reader response journals. Students are asked to read the passage independently. The text, matching activity, comprehension questions, and Madelynn's responses appear below.

Copyright © Mometrix Media. You have been licensed one copy of this document for personal use only. Any other reproduction or redistribution is strictly prohibited. All rights reserved. This content is provided for test preparation purposes only and does not imply an endorsement by Mometrix of any particular political, scientific, or religious point of view.

READING PASSAGE

What you see when you look outside depends on the geography of where you live. **Geography** is the study of the physical and living things on Earth. This simple definition includes many things, including the landforms that make up the Earth's surface. **Landforms** are the natural physical features that we find when we go outside. Different regions of Earth have different kinds of landforms. Some examples of landforms we might find are deserts, plains, mountains, oceans, lakes, rivers, islands, or peninsulas.

Deserts are very dry, hot, and arid areas of land. Very little rain falls in deserts during the year, and because of that, there is very little water. You will not find a lot of vegetation in deserts, either, and only certain kinds of animals can live there. Even though deserts are quite hot during the day, they get very cold at night.

Plains are large, flat areas of land and can be found on all seven continents. Many plains are grassy, but they can also be deserts or forests. **Mountains** can also be found on every continent. These large landforms stretch high above the ground and can be very steep and rocky. Mountains are usually formed over millions of years by pressure created between tectonic plates.

Areas of land that are surrounded by water on all sides are called **islands**. Islands can be found in almost any large body of water, such as oceans, rivers, or even lakes. Many islands are big enough for people to live on them, and some are even their own countries! Some areas of land are only surrounded by water on three sides. These are called **peninsulas**.

Bodies of water are also landforms. The **ocean** is the largest body of salt water on Earth and makes up 98% of all the water on the planet. All other bodies of water eventually lead to the ocean. We have five names for different regions of the ocean. They are called the Atlantic, Pacific, Indian, Arctic, and Antarctic.

Rivers are bodies of fresh water that flow into other bodies of water, such as the ocean. They can be wide or narrow, shallow or deep, and are constantly moving. Rivers are used by people for many purposes, such as fishing, transporting goods, or even drinking! **Lakes** are another type of freshwater body. These bodies of water are surrounded by land and can either be natural or man-made.

Copyright © Mometrix Media. You have been licensed one copy of this document for personal use only. Any other reproduction or redistribution is strictly prohibited. All rights reserved. This content is provided for test preparation purposes only and does not imply an endorsement by Mometrix of any particular political, scientific, or religious point of view.

<u>MATCHING ACTIVITY:</u>

Directions: Match each landform with the correct description.

Landform	Student Choices	Answer Choices
River	**a.**	a. Surrounded completely by water
Peninsula	**f.**	b. Hot, dry, arid area of land
Island	**a.**	c. Largest body of salt water on Earth
Mountain	**h.**	d. Body of water surrounded by land
Lake	**e.**	e. Constantly flowing body of fresh water
Ocean	**c.**	f. Large, flat area of land
Plain	**b.**	g. Land surrounded by water on three sides
Desert	**f.**	h. Tall, steep, rocky landform

Comprehension Questions:

1. What is the definition of landforms?
2. What are the two types of freshwater bodies found on Earth?
3. What do we call different regions of the Earth's Ocean?
4. What are some ways that people use rivers?
5. What are two characteristics of deserts?
6. How are mountains usually formed?

Madelynn's Responses:

1. The difnishin of land forms is antyhing we can find on the land
2. Ocens and also rivirs
3. We can call them ether salt water or frish water
4. Mayb for a boat or to ketch fishes
5. Desrts are awlays hot out
6. By mayb wen a vulkano rupts

Copyright © Mometrix Media. You have been licensed one copy of this document for personal use only. Any other reproduction or redistribution is strictly prohibited. All rights reserved.
This content is provided for test preparation purposes only and does not imply an endorsement by Mometrix of any particular political, scientific, or religious point of view.

Answer Key and Explanations

Multiple Choice Questions

1. A: Verbal dyspraxia refers to trouble with accurately producing sounds due to oral motor functions. Verbal dyspraxia is a broad grouping of motor speech conditions and may present as inaccurate and inconsistent speech, slow speaking, and difficulty in producing sounds accurately in isolation or in typical speech.

2. A: It is beneficial for ELLs to practice phonemic awareness skills on words they know in English. Some English phonemes may not be used in students' native languages. Therefore, introducing English vocabulary words that contain these phonemes helps give these sounds a meaningful context. While phonological and phonemic awareness in students' native languages can be beneficial when they are learning English, it may lead to overgeneralization of rules of the native languages. Therefore, in instructional settings, using familiar words in English will help students practice the phonemes and patterns of English. Students will need to gradually learn phonemes that are not part of their native languages, but it is not ideal to introduce them first. Phonological and phonemic awareness assists with learning the alphabetic principle, so it is beneficial for students to develop these skills first.

3. B: Book concepts refers to knowing how to hold and manipulate books. The preschool student in choice B is holding the book upside down and not turning pages from front to back, indicating she has not yet developed an understanding of book concepts. Choice A demonstrates a student who is relying on the semantic cueing system rather than using a variety of decoding strategies. Choice C demonstrates a student who has not yet mastered return sweep, and choice D demonstrates a student who has not yet mastered one-to-one correspondence.

4. B: Educational research into teaching practices for nonverbal communication is notably lacking; however, teachers who have experimented with lessons (cf. Darn, 2014) have discovered it is best to teach nonverbal communication skills in small chunks (A), using appropriate situations (B) wherein the context of the theme or situation is congruent with the language. They also find that to help students use gestures and expressions to reinforce linguistic meaning, teachers must include drama-based instructional activities that build student confidence (C) and creativity (D).

5. D: When students take away a sound in a word and say what new word they are left with, they are practicing phoneme deletion. Onset and rime manipulation involve breaking or combining a word between the first sound and the remainder of the word. Segmenting involves breaking a word into its individual sounds. Phoneme isolation involves identifying a specific phoneme within a word.

6. C: Readers use the syntactic cueing system when they consider sentence structure and grammar to decode unknown words. Alex is substituting a word that sounds right in the sentence. If Alex were using the graphophonic cueing system, he would choose a word that is structurally similar to the existing word, such as a word that starts with the same sound. If Alex were using the semantic cueing system, he would use picture cues or prior knowledge to guess the word. The pragmatic cueing system refers to consideration of the purposes of reading in given situations.

7. C: Word sorts assist students with comparing and contrasting features of words. While completing the sort, students must analyze each word to determine and categorize its vowel sound and determine how each word is similar to and different from other words in the set. Segmenting

25

Copyright © Mometrix Media. You have been licensed one copy of this document for personal use only. Any other reproduction or redistribution is strictly prohibited. All rights reserved.
This content is provided for test preparation purposes only and does not imply an endorsement by Mometrix of any particular political, scientific, or religious point of view.

words using Elkonin boxes helps students break words into individual phonemes, but it doesn't assist with comparing and contrasting. Tracing words may help students practice short vowel spelling patterns, but it doesn't assist with comparing and contrasting either. Including words with short vowel sounds on the weekly spelling list will mainly assist with learning spelling patterns.

8. C: When a word can be pronounced two different ways, reading the sentence twice and pronouncing the word each way can help the reader determine which pronunciation makes sense. For example, a student might encounter a sentence that says, "The mother put a bow in her daughter's hair." Knowing that *bow* can be pronounced two different ways, the student can read the sentence twice, pronouncing the word differently each time. That strategy should help the student identify which way makes sense. Choices A and B are incorrect because identifying known parts of the word using visual clues will not assist the reader with knowing which pronunciation is correct in the given context. Additional context clues from the surrounding text are needed. Choice D is incorrect because the student may know other *oo* words with both pronunciations, so again, additional context clues are needed.

9. B: Experts find that narrating ELL students' actions, i.e., linguistic encoding, helps encourage them to speak English (A), that teachers should assign activities that include hands-on learning (B), and that the activities they assign should be meaningful (C). They also find that teachers should focus on which language function the students must apply to complete a lesson, not just that they complete it (D).

10. A: Recent research shows that dyslexia and similar reading difficulties are primarily neurodevelopmental in origin, i.e., mainly due to both neurological and developmental rather than environmental factors. (Environmental deprivation of early exposure to reading activities can delay literacy development, but most [85 percent of] diagnosed learning problems are related primarily to difficulties with reading and other language skills.)

11. A: Rhyming is a component of phonological awareness, which is the ability to identify and manipulate sounds in spoken words. Nursery rhymes are a common way to introduce young children to rhymes and help them develop phonological awareness skills. Identifying rhyming words does not require children to identify or manipulate sounds at the phoneme level, so it does not involve phonemic awareness. Additionally, it does not involve connecting the sounds to the letters that produce them, so it does not involve the alphabetic principle or phonics.

12. C: Children often invent spellings during early learning. Though vowels are needed to decode words, these invented spellings frequently omit vowels (A); therefore, children need a great deal of practice to hear vowel sounds in words. Children can discriminate long vowel sounds more easily than short vowel sounds, not vice versa (B). Hence (though many phonics programs start with short vowels), phonological discrimination exercises should focus on discriminating long vowels before short vowels, not vice versa (D).

13. D: Research shows that phonics instruction is more effective than no phonics instruction, and also that it is more effective when it is systematic and explicit then when it is not (A). Research also shows that it is equally effective for children of all socioeconomic levels (B), that it is more effective when introduced in kindergarten or first grade (C), and that it is more effective when it helps students understand why they are learning letter-sound relationships and helps them apply this learning (D) to reading and writing.

14. D: Pragmatics refers to understanding the social rules of communication, including the ability to adjust the level of formality to match a specific social situation. Morphology refers to understanding

Copyright © Mometrix Media. You have been licensed one copy of this document for personal use only. Any other reproduction or redistribution is strictly prohibited. All rights reserved. This content is provided for test preparation purposes only and does not imply an endorsement by Mometrix of any particular political, scientific, or religious point of view.

word parts and word forms. Semantics refers to understanding the meanings of words. Syntax refers to understanding grammar and sentence structure.

15. B: Explicit and systematic phonics instruction involves planning the teaching of specific phonics skills in a logical order, from simplest to most complex, using a part-to-whole approach. It requires understanding students' existing phonics knowledge and planning instruction to address specific skills that they still need to develop. Choice A and choice D demonstrate implicit phonics instruction, where students read whole texts, and phonics instruction occurs based on students' struggles and/or observations as they read. It uses a whole-to-part approach. Choice C involves preplanned phonics instruction, but the teacher is selecting phonics skills to address based on the content of the books rather than a research-based sequencing of skills from simplest to most complex.

16. B: Explicit phonics instruction uses a part-to-whole approach. Mr. Clark's students first learn the *st* blend in isolation before applying it to whole words. Implicit phonics instruction, also referred to as whole language or analytical phonics, uses a whole-to-part approach. Students recognize whole words by sight before breaking them down into individual phonemes.

17. A: An inflectional ending is a letter or group of letters added to the end of a root word. It is sometimes used to change the tense of the root word, as in the case of adding *ed* to *jump* to indicate past tense. Both *-ed* and *-ing* are inflectional endings. The words in choice B end in diphthongs, which are formed when two vowel sounds are combined within a syllable. The words in choice C end in consonant digraphs, or two or more consonants that are combined to form a new sound. The words in choice D rhyme, and they use different spelling patterns to make the same sound.

18. C: The student has spelled all of the words correctly except for those with silent letters. Therefore, it would be most helpful to focus on silent-letter spelling patterns. Additionally, the student had no errors in subject/verb agreement.

19. A: The "guess the word" game described teaches the phonological process of blending phonemes, i.e., combining individual speech sounds into whole words. Deleting phonemes (B) would involve having students change words by removing one speech sound from each word to create a new one, e.g., from "brat" to "bat." Segmenting phonemes (C) would involve separating words into their individual component phonemes, e.g., "sun" to "s," "u," and "n." Substituting phonemes (D) would involve changing words by replacing one phoneme in each word with another, e.g., from "sun" to "fun."

20. B: In order to teach segmentation, i.e., separating linguistic units into their component parts, on multiple phonological levels, the educator must teach students to separate sentences (a higher level) into their component words (A) and to separate words (the next level down) into their component syllables, or into their onsets (initial phonemes) and rimes (following phoneme groups) (C). They must also teach students to separate syllables into their individual phonemes (D). Whereas choice B includes multiple phonological levels, the other choices only address one phonological level each.

21. D: When young children recognize environmental print, they learn that print contains meaning. For example, a child who recognizes a familiar fast-food sign understands that the words represent the restaurant name. Children often recognize environmental print before learning specific letter names and letter/sound relationships. Additionally, environmental print often contains complex spelling patterns and is difficult for beginning readers to decode. Environmental print does not

Copyright © Mometrix Media. You have been licensed one copy of this document for personal use only. Any other reproduction or redistribution is strictly prohibited. All rights reserved.
This content is provided for test preparation purposes only and does not imply an endorsement by Mometrix of any particular political, scientific, or religious point of view.

teach one-to-one correspondence unless someone reads the print while simultaneously pointing to each individual word.

22. D: Multisyllabic words often contain smaller parts that students recognize, such as prefixes, roots, and suffixes. Identifying these known parts can help students figure out the words. Context clues can help students guess words that make sense, but students should be able to apply word analysis skills to cross check their guesses and ensure they are selecting the correct words. Stretching out the sounds and blending the phonemes are helpful strategies for decoding shorter words with predictable spelling patterns. However, these strategies are less reliable for decoding multisyllabic words with more complex spelling patterns.

23. B: The word *chain* contains a common consonant digraph, *ch*; and two vowels together, *ai*, which make the /ā/ sound. Recognizing these patterns will make the word easy to sound out. In choice A, the two vowels in *tear* do not make the /ē/ sound, as would likely be expected. The sound produced by *ain* in *curtain* makes it more difficult for a first grader to sound out, as does the sound of the *c* in *ocean*.

24. A: The student is using both the picture in the book and his prior knowledge to make sense of the text, which demonstrates use of the semantic cueing system. When using the syntactic cueing system, readers select words that sound right using knowledge of grammar and sentence structure. When readers use the graphophonic cueing system, they use knowledge of letter/sound relationships to decode words. When using pragmatic cues, readers consider their purposes for reading in given situations.

25. A: Concepts of print are conventions used to convey meaning in printed text. They include locating the title and author's name, holding the book correctly, tracking print, reading from left to right, and other similar concepts. Phonological awareness is the ability to identify and manipulate sounds in spoken words, and phonemic awareness is the ability to identify and manipulate sounds at the phoneme level. Close reading is a strategy where students deeply analyze texts to increase comprehension.

26. D: Alphabetic principle is the understanding that each letter makes a predictable sound. Students are practicing the alphabetic principle by matching the letter to a word that begins with the sound that letter makes. Encoding is the process of translating phonemes to graphemes, or recording sounds using letters. One-to-one correspondence is the understanding that each printed word corresponds with one spoken word. Phoneme isolation is the identification of the beginning, middle, or ending sound in a word.

27. C: When students reread familiar texts, they do not need to exert energy on decoding unfamiliar words. As a result, more energy is available to focus on fluency, including phrasing and expression. Choral reading allows students to match their reading rate and expression with others in the group who are modeling fluent reading, including the teacher. Reading new texts requires students to spend more energy on decoding and comprehension, which may interfere with fluency. Audio versions of texts can serve as models of fluent reading, but students still need opportunities to practice. Partner reading may be helpful if students are matched with fluent readers, but this is not guaranteed.

28. B: Closed syllables end with consonants and show readers places where words can be divided during decoding. By dividing the words into syllables, Laura can sound out *rab-bit* and *prob-lem* more easily. Open syllables end with vowels, and these words do not contain open syllables. If Laura divides the words into sections with CVCC spelling patterns, she will not be dividing them

Copyright © Mometrix Media. You have been licensed one copy of this document for personal use only. Any other reproduction or redistribution is strictly prohibited. All rights reserved. This content is provided for test preparation purposes only and does not imply an endorsement by Mometrix of any particular political, scientific, or religious point of view.

into syllables, which will make decoding more difficult. Double consonants occur when the same consonant appears twice in a row in a word. Although *rabbit* has a double consonant (the two *b's*), *problem* does not.

29. C: Choice C best demonstrates an intensive intervention plan because it includes small-group, targeted instruction at frequent, regularly scheduled times. The remaining options can assist the student with learning consonant blends, but they do not include frequent, regularly scheduled teacher interactions. During these intervention times, the teacher can provide instruction, supervise practice opportunities, offer feedback, monitor progress, and more.

30. D: It offers a systematic approach to untangling the wide variety of vowel sounds when an unfamiliar word is encountered. Code knowledge, also called orthographic tendencies, is a helpful approach to decoding a word when multiple pronunciation possibilities exist. For example, in the words *toe, go, though,* and *low*, the long O sound is written in a variety of ways. A code knowledge approach teaches a reader to first try a short vowel sound. If that doesn't help, the reader should consider the different ways the vowel or vowel groups can be pronounced, based on what he knows about other words.

31. B: Introducing sound-spellings (A) is for teaching students which written letters correspond to which spoken sounds, which they must know *before* learning to decode words. Discriminating individual phonemes within words (C) is for teaching students phonological awareness, which they also must have *before* decoding new words. Reviewing sound-spellings to overlearn them (D) is for phonics maintenance rather than word decoding. Blending phonemes into words (B) is for helping students learn a strategy to apply their sound-spelling learning to decoding unfamiliar words.

32. C: Researchers have found that not all children benefit from instruction in phonological awareness (A), even though most children do. Children at risk for speech or language delays do not benefit most (B); studies providing this instruction have shown that almost one-third of at-risk children realized little or no improvement. But the benefits are not limited to children with normal language development (D), either. Some of these researchers have concluded the instruction must be more intensive or explicit for at-risk students.

33. C: Final blending individually identifies and pronounces each phoneme in a word before blending them. This helps teachers identify specific problem areas: some students may give the wrong sound for a letter; others may identify letter-sounds correctly without blending (e.g., pronouncing /sa/ as "suh-ah," not "sah"). Successive blending (A) pronounces individual phonemes sequentially; teachers first prolong (e.g., "ssssuuuunnnn"), then gradually shorten prolonged phonemes ("sssuuunnn," "ssuunn," "sun"). Teachers help students eventually transition from blending aloud to silent blending (B). Line blending (D) cumulatively reviews word sets and sentences already taught until students can blend independently.

34. C: CVC words, which contain a consonant, a short vowel, and another consonant, are typically taught before the other listed spelling patterns. These words are easy to decode for beginning readers. Long vowel sounds, such as those in choices A and B, are typically taught after short vowel sounds. Additionally, consonant blends and digraphs, as found in choice D, are also typically taught after CVC words.

35. B: On a continuum, the simplest level of phonological awareness is represented by being able to recognize and produce rhymes in songs, and show understanding that sentences contain individual words by segmenting them (D). Segmenting words into syllables and blending syllables into words (A) represents a more complex level around the middle of the continuum. A higher level of

29

Copyright © Mometrix Media. You have been licensed one copy of this document for personal use only. Any other reproduction or redistribution is strictly prohibited. All rights reserved.
This content is provided for test preparation purposes only and does not imply an endorsement by Mometrix of any particular political, scientific, or religious point of view.

complexity is segmenting words into onsets and rimes and blending onsets and rimes into words (C). The highest level is phonemic awareness, i.e., understanding that words contain individual phonemes and being able to manipulate (blend, segment, delete, substitute) these (B).

36. C: The three cueing systems are the graphophonic (spelling-to-sound relationships), syntactic, and semantic. Grammar (A), word order (B), and sentence structure (D) belong in the category of the syntactic cueing system. Word meaning (C) belongs in the category of the semantic cueing system.

37. C: While it is true that phonemic awareness is a listening and speaking skill rather than a reading and writing skill (A), it is equally true that children develop phonemic awareness better when instruction combines print with speech sounds (B). This helps children realize how speech sounds and printed letters connect and apply this insight. However, just including print is not sufficient (C). Teachers should also point to printed letters while saying them aloud to draw children's attention to sound-letter connections (D).

38. A: Students with dyslexia tend to perform much worse than their intelligence and knowledge would indicate on objective formats like multiple-choice tests. They are likely to have *equal* amounts of difficulty with reading short function words (e.g., *an, on, in*) as with reading long, multisyllabic words (B). While they do have trouble with fluid thinking, e.g., thinking "on the spot" to produce spoken and/or written verbal responses, they also have equal difficulty with retaining and/or retrieving names, dates, random lists, phone numbers, and other information through rote memorization and recall (C). Students with dyslexia typically have more trouble understanding words in isolation than in context (D), because they rely on the surrounding context to comprehend word meanings.

39. D: The alphabetic principle is the concept that printed letters and letter combinations correspond to speech sounds. In order to learn the sounds that alphabet letters represent, children must first know the names of the letters. First they learn letter names, then they learn the shapes of the letters (A), and then they learn the sounds indicated by the letters (B). They learn each of these in sequence rather than all at the same time (C).

40. D: Research-based recommendations from the COI include teaching students how to use effective reading comprehension strategies—as well as giving them supportive practice in using them—throughout the school day (a); setting and sustaining high standards for text, vocabulary, AND questions and conversation (b); focusing equally on raising student motivation to read and student engagement with reading (c); and instructing students in the content knowledge they need to master concepts crucial to their comprehension and learning (d).

41. B: Among the answer choices provided, the best option for helping students pronounce new words is to encourage students to sound out the words slowly, keeping the rules of vowels and consonants in mind. This is not, of course, the only option for assisting students with word pronunciation, but it is the best option among the available choices for this question.

42. A: Letter–sound correspondence relies on the relationship between a spoken sound or group of sounds and the letters conventionally used in English to write them.

43. B: Students must be able to distinguish between printed words and the spaces between them to identify the first and last letters of each word, as spaces are the boundaries between words. It is not true that all normally developing students can tell words from spaces: those not exposed to or familiar with print media may need to be taught this distinction. Although left-to-right directionality is more of a problem for ELL students whose L1s have different writing or printing

Copyright © Mometrix Media. You have been licensed one copy of this document for personal use only. Any other reproduction or redistribution is strictly prohibited. All rights reserved.
This content is provided for test preparation purposes only and does not imply an endorsement by Mometrix of any particular political, scientific, or religious point of view.

directions (e.g., some Asian languages are written vertically, some can be written vertically or horizontally, and some Semitic languages like Hebrew and Arabic are written right-to-left), again, children unfamiliar with print or writing may also not know writing, print, or book directionality either. Identifying basic punctuation is important to reading comprehension as it affects meaning. For example, consider "Let's eat, Grandma" vs. "Let's eat Grandma"—one comma differentiates an invitation to dinner from a cannibalistic proposal.

44. C: Children develop phonological awareness through a combination of incidental learning via being naturally exposed to language in their environments, and receiving direct instruction from adults. They do not develop it solely through one or the other, or neither.

45. A: Metacognition is the ability to "think about thinking," or the ability to reflect on, analyze, and understand one's own thinking processes. Through the process approach to writing, students learn how to evaluate their own writing in more objective and constructive ways. In the process approach, students interact more often and consistently with their peers while writing. This element of student interactions is more related to collaboration and social skills than metacognition. Another element of process writing is the identification of authentic audiences: knowing for whom they are writing helps students focus on achieving specific purposes and identifying which kinds of reasoning, logic, tone, and word choice to appeal to those audiences. This is more other-oriented than metacognitive or self-oriented. Process writing also includes the element of personal student responsibility for writing. Such ownership enables greater independence in student choices, craft, practice, and motivation more than self-analysis of cognitive processes.

46. B: This is an example of a closed question because the student can only answer "simile" or "metaphor" without needing to elaborate unless asked to explain the answer. In contrast, choice C is an open-ended question because the student must both define simile and metaphor and explain the difference between them. Choice A is an open-ended literature question because the student cannot answer with yes, no, or some other single word or short phrase; he or she has to describe the action or events in a story that represent its climax, which requires understanding story structure, story elements, knowing the definition of a story's climax, reading the story, and understanding it. Choice D is a very open-ended question, as students have considerable latitude in giving the reasons each of them perceives for having poetry.

47. A: Cognates are words in different languages that share the same roots, such as the English word *conflict* and the Spanish word *conflicto*. If students know the meanings of the words in their native languages, they can apply that knowledge to determine the meanings of the English words. Realia are everyday objects that provide visual representations of words, also contributing to vocabulary development. While recognizing known parts in cognates can assist students with decoding new words quickly, it is less likely to assist with prosody. Phonological and phonemic awareness have to do with identifying and manipulating sounds in words rather than identifying word meanings or related spelling patterns.

48. C: Aesthetic response refers to a reader's personal interactions with a text. Rather than recalling information about the text, aesthetic response is personalized and based on the reader's own thoughts, feelings, and reactions. Choice C asks the readers to describe how a certain part of the story made them feel; therefore, it is focused on their aesthetic responses to the text. The other questions can be answered using information contained within the story rather than the readers' own personal reactions.

31

Copyright © Mometrix Media. You have been licensed one copy of this document for personal use only. Any other reproduction or redistribution is strictly prohibited. All rights reserved. This content is provided for test preparation purposes only and does not imply an endorsement by Mometrix of any particular political, scientific, or religious point of view.

49. A: To help students use textual evidence to support their answers, they should be taught to locate the evidence directly in the text rather than relying on memory. One strategy that addresses this skill is underlining the information within the text when it is located. Rereading the text multiple times may help students remember the information contained in the text, but it does not encourage them to locate the specific answers to questions. Reading and eliminating answer choices is a beneficial test-taking strategy in general, but it does not assist students with locating and verifying specific details. A story map helps to identify key information in the story, but there is no guarantee that it will address any specific test questions.

50. D: If the student is having difficulties with comprehension rather than decoding, he will likely benefit from having the information represented in multiple ways. Seeing visual representations of the words and content may assist him with comprehension. Additionally, multimedia textbooks often contain features like hyperlinked vocabulary words that display definitions when clicked. Choices A and B would only read the same vocabulary words aloud without any additional explanation or visuals to assist with comprehension. An outline also presents the information in text rather than focusing on visual clues.

51. D: Schema theory suggests that when people encounter new concepts, the newly learned knowledge gets organized into units called schemata. When they encounter related information in the future, they access their existing schemata to make sense of it. Therefore, a KWL chart, which helps students relate a topic to existing knowledge, best supports schema theory. The remaining types of graphic organizers support reading development but do not specifically require students to activate prior knowledge.

52. B: The student is monitoring his own reading and recognizing when something doesn't make sense. When he realizes that something doesn't make sense, he knows he has likely made an error. Monitoring one's own reading is a metacognitive skill. Decoding refers to the process of translating printed words into spoken words. Evaluative skills refer to the ability to evaluate something using evidence and/or prior knowledge. Application skills refer to the ability to apply skills in different contexts.

53. B: Manipulatives are three-dimensional concrete objects that students can not only look at but also manipulate, as the name indicates (e.g., touch, move, rearrange, dismantle, reassemble). Examples may be three-dimensional objects, demonstrations, or (more often) verbal descriptions given orally, printed, or written. Graphic organizers are diagrams (e.g., Venn diagrams), charts, timelines, concept maps, word webs, etc., which are two-dimensional, visual, graphic materials. Charts, tables, and graphs, though less pictorial and conceptual and more linear and numerical than graphic organizers, are also two-dimensional in print, online, or on screen.

54. C: The words in this set can be grouped into two categories: academic vocabulary and content vocabulary. Academic vocabulary words are commonly used in school but are not specific to one subject area. For example, students may compare shapes in math, compare living things in science, and compare characters in reading. Content vocabulary refers to words related to one specific subject area. *Organism*, *cell*, and *habitat* are typically used in science.

55. A: Introducing new vocabulary words will help students decode the words faster when they are encountered in the text, thus assisting with fluency. Recognizing the words and knowing their meanings will also build readers' confidence. Additionally, explaining the meanings of the words in advance will help students comprehend the text when they read it independently. Reading the first few pages aloud without discussion will not help students recognize or understand the vocabulary words, nor will it highlight important words beyond the first few pages. Listing what students want

Copyright © Mometrix Media. You have been licensed one copy of this document for personal use only. Any other reproduction or redistribution is strictly prohibited. All rights reserved. This content is provided for test preparation purposes only and does not imply an endorsement by Mometrix of any particular political, scientific, or religious point of view.

to learn about the topic helps to set a purpose for reading, not explain vocabulary. Predicting helps students activate prior knowledge, make connections, and stay actively engaged in the reading process.

56. D: Choice D includes a prediction because the student tells what she thinks is going to happen in the story. She also includes text evidence by explaining how the clue at the end of the chapter influenced her prediction. Choice A shows the student describing the theme of the story. Choice B includes a prediction, but the student has supported it with a personal connection rather than using text evidence. Choice C shows the student's explanation of the author's purpose for writing the story.

57. B: Experts advise that to differentiate reading instruction, teachers should not just reserve read-aloud materials for fun, but use them as common teaching texts (A) for building background knowledge, demonstrating strategy application, introducing issues, and inviting students to journal responses to issues, enabling all students to access needed reading skills and information. They should teach units using multiple texts to meet diverse reading levels (B); reserve 15-30 minutes at least three times a week for independent practice reading at student comfort levels (C); and organize units around topics, issues, or genres instead of basing them on the text (D).

58. B: Teachers should instruct typically developing students in grades K-2 in capitalizing the initial letter of the first word of every sentence in written compositions. They should teach capitalization of the initial letters of salutations and closings in letters (A), names of months and weekdays (C), and names of holidays and countries (D) to typically developing students in grades 3-5.

59. B: Including a word bank assists struggling readers with completing the activity by providing them with options to choose from. It is a way of scaffolding the activity while still requiring students to use context clues to determine which word is the best fit in each sentence. Providing the first few letters of each answer offers a bigger hint and may allow the student to guess the word easily. Cloze reading activities can be done in pairs, but it is possible that one student may supply the answer for the struggling reader. It is also possible for struggling readers to complete more than three questions with appropriate scaffolding.

60. B: Caleb is stating that nobody likes meatloaf after observing that a small sample of the school population does not appear to like it. He is drawing conclusions based on insufficient data, which is an overgeneralization. An illogical conclusion occurs when someone draws conclusions about the relationships between two things without data supporting the relationship. Personal bias occurs when conclusions are based on personal opinions rather than data. Circular reasoning occurs when someone supports a claim by restating the same claim rather than by providing new data.

61. C: The teacher is demonstrating a think-aloud, or sharing her thinking process as she uses a reading strategy. In this example, she explains her thoughts as she uses context clues to determine the meaning of an unknown word. Mental images and visualizations both refer to the pictures that readers get in their minds when they read. Predictions are logical guesses about what might happen in a text.

62. D: Synthesis involves gathering information from multiple sources and combining it to make meaning, as students are doing when they write their research reports on sustainable farming practices. As students collect information from each source, they also consider how their initial thoughts on the topic have changed. Evaluating involves making a judgment about something. Inferring involves using clues in the text to make meaning rather than using information that is directly stated. Drawing conclusions involves making judgements based on inferences.

Copyright © Mometrix Media. You have been licensed one copy of this document for personal use only. Any other reproduction or redistribution is strictly prohibited. All rights reserved.
This content is provided for test preparation purposes only and does not imply an endorsement by Mometrix of any particular political, scientific, or religious point of view.

63. C: Motivation, i.e., how interested students are in reading and in what ways (e.g., genres, subject matter, reading levels, etc.), is a psychological factor that influences not only whether or how much students read but also their comprehension. Attention (A) is a prerequisite for comprehension, problems with visual and auditory perception (C) can cause reading problems, and working memory (D) is required for word decoding and reading comprehension. Unlike motivation, these three are all cognitive factors.

64. B: When students learn to summarize text, they learn to identify the most important ideas in a text AND organize those ideas in their minds (a); identify the themes, problems, and solutions in the text (b); monitor reading comprehension; AND correctly sequence (c) story events, essay points, etc. Graphic organizers, drawing, and other visuals help students visualize connections more than summarizing (d), a more mental and verbal than visual activity (though such visualization can aid summarization).

65. C: Understanding text features can help students locate key information in nonfiction texts. Additionally, understanding how different types of nonfiction texts are typically organized provides predictability and structure when reading new texts, which can assist with comprehension. While rereading and summarizing can be effective, asking the student to locate key information without any additional guidance or scaffolding is less likely to be effective. Story maps, which help students identify story elements, are used to assist with comprehending fictional texts.

66. C: A complex sentence has at least one dependent and one independent clause. A dependent clause cannot stand alone as a sentence, while an independent clause can. In choice C, the dependent clause is, "Before going to school"; while the independent clause is, "Michael brushed his teeth." Choice A is a simple sentence containing one independent clause. Choice B is a sentence with a compound predicate. Choice D is a compound sentence, meaning it contains two or more independent clauses joined by a coordinating conjunction or semicolon.

67. B: Students reflect in reader response journals after independent, not sustained silent, reading (A). Teachers can use journals to monitor student reading, check comprehension, discuss texts, and suggest additional books (B). Not all students know how to respond to text by writing. Teachers should initially model the process, including prompts, and post lists of these, model methods for generating personal topics without prompts through the year, and give students lists of these for reference (C) to keep in their journals. Teachers should advise students to read about 80 percent of the time and write about 20 percent of the time (D).

68. A: By demonstrating or using think-alouds, the teacher should first model identifying and recording (e.g.) three research questions, then referring to the table of contents and headings in a text selected for this purpose, then reading chapters identified from the previous step for pertinent information, and then classifying or categorizing the information he or she has found according to which of the three questions it answers.

69. A: Teacher "think-alouds" using text the students are reading reflect the explicit instruction component of modeling, i.e., the teacher demonstrates how to use a comprehension strategy. Before modeling, the teacher should use direct explanation (D) to inform students why or how a strategy aids comprehension and when to use it. After modeling, the teacher helps students learn when and how to use the strategy through guided practice (C). Then the teacher helps students practice applying it (B) until they can do so independently.

70. B: A phoneme (A) is an individual speech sound. A grapheme (C) is an individual written symbol, like an alphabet letter or punctuation mark. A sememe (D) is the meaning carried by a

Copyright © Mometrix Media. You have been licensed one copy of this document for personal use only. Any other reproduction or redistribution is strictly prohibited. All rights reserved. This content is provided for test preparation purposes only and does not imply an endorsement by Mometrix of any particular political, scientific, or religious point of view.

morpheme; e.g., the -s at the end of a noun is a morpheme; its sememe is pluralization. A morpheme (B) is the smallest individual meaningful grammatical unit that cannot be broken down further; -*tion* is thus a single morpheme, though it contains multiple phonemes and graphemes. Its sememe might be called verb nominalization.

71. A: In choice A, the teacher guides previewing of information to show students how to put themselves in the right frame of mind to listen carefully for meaning. Students are then able to listen in a guided way based upon the previewing. By varying the type of comprehension assessment, the teacher will get a better understanding of what the students learned. Choice B is a good exercise but does not provide for direct instruction by the teacher or a particularly skilled student. In Choice C, students are focusing more on reading comprehension than listening since they must read the story to themselves and then write a report. There is then no way to gauge what they have learned. Choice D would be useful but does not include teacher-guided previewing, which is very helpful in building comprehension.

72. B: Word associations require a student to pull from previous knowledge or experience. For example, if the student is presented with the word *aardvark* but has never seen or heard of an aardvark, he or she will not be able to make associations. While word association may be a good activity for students after they have reviewed the vocabulary words, it may be counterproductive if the students are unfamiliar with the words. Teachers should also be mindful of cultural differences that may account for a variation in previous knowledge.

73. A: Alphabet books, wordless picture books, and easy-to-read books all promote skills important for children beginning to become readers. The other genres are more suitable for older children with well-developed reading skills.

74. C: The most helpful strategy for discerning which of two homonyms (sound-alike words) is correct without knowing the spelling is its surrounding context of the sentence, paragraph, and/or book and subject matter. For example, "Mexico cedes land" and "Mexico seeds land" sound the same, but if the context continues "to the United States," the meaning of "cedes" applies. Pictures (A) help children identify unknown words rather than differentiate homonyms. Phonics (B) help students sound out unfamiliar words, not differentiate meanings. Grammar (D) can help when one homonym is a verb and the other a noun, for example; but "cedes" and "seeds" are the same part of speech with different meanings, so grammar alone does not help as much as context.

75. A: The student should receive instruction focused on just the areas in which he is exhibiting difficulty, which are comprehension and vocabulary. Improved vocabulary will give him greater skill at comprehending the meaning of a particular text. Strategies focused on enhancing comprehension together with a stronger vocabulary will provide the greatest help.

76. C: Many factors can affect a student's ability to understand what he or she is reading. Building comprehension skills is an ongoing process and can be made difficult if a student lacks the appropriate level of reading fluency. If he or she cannot read accurately or with enough speed, he or she will have much more trouble with comprehension than the average student. It is important to identify any decoding or vocabulary problems that might be affecting comprehension first; if those can be solved, comprehension skills may naturally increase as reading fluency increases.

77. A: Narrative writing is storytelling, as opposed to expository or informational writing. Ability to retell the story is a key strategy for assessing a student's reading comprehension. Decoding new words (B), inventing original spellings for new words (C), and identifying and producing rhymes

Copyright © Mometrix Media. You have been licensed one copy of this document for personal use only. Any other reproduction or redistribution is strictly prohibited. All rights reserved.
This content is provided for test preparation purposes only and does not imply an endorsement by Mometrix of any particular political, scientific, or religious point of view.

(D) are all abilities whereby teachers can assess student skills for decoding printed words, but not their comprehension of printed text.

78. B: A KWL chart allows students to list, before they read, what they **K**now about a subject; what they **W**ant to know or learn about it; and, after reading, what they have **L**earned about it. This is a good example of a research-based instructional strategy for activating students' prior knowledge. The teacher giving the students background information is the opposite of finding out what they already know. The teacher asking students what they know about the subject after they have read a text is also the opposite of the goal. Activating prior knowledge before reading enables students to build upon what they already know when they begin reading, as successful readers do, versus beginning to read without thinking, as less successful readers do. Similarly, the teacher should ask students their opinions and reactions about a topic before they read, not after, to activate their existing knowledge.

79. C: Choice A is an example of a student reading strategy based primarily on using grammatical cues to meaning: verbs are modified by adverbs. Choice B is an example of using semantic cues to meaning: "horrible" more likely modifies "disaster," "mess," "mistake," etc., than "happiness," "celebration," "opportunity," etc. Choice C is an example of using syntactic cues to meaning: in English, standard word order dictates that adjectives precede nouns. Choice D is an example of decoding difficulties or reading only one word at a time, which interfere with student reading strategies using grammatical, syntactic, or semantic cues to meaning.

80. B: Informal assessments can consist of everyday activities, such as grading homework, observing students, taking anecdotal records, and talking to students about their learning. Therefore, the results are not standardized, making it difficult to compare results among groups or over time. The other options describe limitations of formal assessments, which may increase student anxiety and can be more expensive and time consuming to implement and score.

81. A: Rubrics are a type of evaluation tool that assign both overall scores and scores in individual component areas of an assignment. In each component area, the criteria used to assign scores for different levels of mastery are outlined. Therefore, students can see their overall grades on assignments, as well as how they performed in each component area. This helps students assess their strengths and weaknesses. Rubrics do not specifically track progress over time, though teachers could evaluate students using the same rubric at different points of the year and compare the results. Rubrics assess individual performance and do not compare students to their peers. Choice D describes a miscue analysis, which is a different type of assessment.

82. B: Fluent readers are able to recognize and understand words at the same time (A). While they recognize words more automatically and quickly, they also comprehend overall meaning, enabling them to use natural, conversational expression accordingly. Hence, students who read aloud in expressionless monotones, despite speed and automaticity, do not read fluently (B). This is typically because they must decode individual words, whereas fluent readers organize words into chunks of meaningful information (C). Whereas non-fluent readers read laboriously, fluent readers read effortlessly (D).

83. B: When a test's items minimize guessing by students (A) through being written clearly, this is a way of determining that the assessment is reliable, not valid (A). Tests with relatively large numbers of items (C) and tests that yield consistent scores over time (D) through repeated administrations are also likely to be reliable. Tests with items measuring the construct that the test claims to measure (B) meet the overall definition of test validity.

Copyright © Mometrix Media. You have been licensed one copy of this document for personal use only. Any other reproduction or redistribution is strictly prohibited. All rights reserved.
This content is provided for test preparation purposes only and does not imply an endorsement by Mometrix of any particular political, scientific, or religious point of view.

84. B: To adhere to basic educational measurement principles as they apply to reading assessment, the first thing schools must do is to set goals. Second, they must adopt standards, defining what students should be able to do and know at specified levels; standards should be written to enable students to meet goals previously set. Third, they must design reading curricula enabling teachers to help students meet standards previously adopted. Fourth, they must develop assessments to measure student progress toward meeting those standards. Designing tests that measure student achievement accurately depends on this sequence.

85. D: Testing instrument reliability is indicated if the test yields consistent results across repeated administrations. Measuring the specific skill that it claims to measure (A) indicates test validity, not reliability. Tests with clearly written items are typically more reliable than those using open-ended, ambiguous questions (B). Tests that measure a skill using a fairly large quantity of items are typically more reliable than tests using only a few, very focused items (C).

86. D: Using quotation marks around quotations, and around certain types of titles, is an appropriate goal for students in grades 3-5. Using periods after declarative sentences (A), using question marks after interrogative sentences (B), and using commas to divide series of words (C) are all appropriate benchmarks for students in grades K-2.

87. C: Although teachers may supply the possible options, students are typically given choices about the books they read for literature circles. This helps maintain interest and engagement throughout the process. Students participate in literature circles in small groups, and there are usually multiple books being read and discussed throughout a classroom. Students are encouraged to lead the discussions and introduce questions and topics for analysis. Additionally, groups may change frequently as students finish books and move on to new texts.

88. C: In this type of ELP standard, third-grade ELLs should understand and follow one-step directions at the beginning level, two- to three-step directions at the early intermediate level, three- to four-step directions at the intermediate and early advanced level, and multiple-step directions at the advanced level (A). They should also be able to follow directions for movement in space relative to position at the beginning, early intermediate, and intermediate levels; and relative to position, frequency, and duration at the early advanced and advanced levels (B). Therefore, (D) is incorrect.

89. B: Some educators (cf. Rheinschild, "Pyramid Reading") order basic literary analysis skills in a hierarchy of progressive difficulty, illustrated in a pyramid (similar in conception to Maslow's hierarchy of needs pyramid, from basic to advanced). As they are progressive, teachers should teach one skill at a time until students master it before moving up to the next (A) rather than trying to cover them all together (B), and throughout the school year should frequently re-teach all the skills using materials of progressively greater complexity (C).

90. D: Books with illustrations (a) combine verbal and nonlinguistic visual media only. "Books on Tape" represent auditory media only. Following in the text as the teacher reads it aloud (c) combines mainly verbal and auditory, and some visual stimuli. Electronic text including audio, visual, touchscreen, and interactive features (d) combines verbal, visual, auditory, and tactile media, plus more active reader participation and immediate feedback.

91. A: This student needs carefully organized lessons in decoding, sight words, vocabulary, and comprehension at least three to five times a week. These mini-lessons must be extremely clear, with the parts broken down to the lowest common denominator. The more tightly interwoven and systematized the instruction, the better chance this student will have. This type of learner needs, first and foremost, instruction that has been highly organized into a system that will make sense to

Copyright © Mometrix Media. You have been licensed one copy of this document for personal use only. Any other reproduction or redistribution is strictly prohibited. All rights reserved.
This content is provided for test preparation purposes only and does not imply an endorsement by Mometrix of any particular political, scientific, or religious point of view.

her. If possible, she should receive private instruction on a daily basis. The instruction needs to focus on decoding, recognizing words, reading with increasing fluency, enhancing vocabulary, and comprehension. She should be working at the Instructional level, or with texts she can read with at least 90% accuracy.

92. C: Teachers need to advise students that when they take research notes on information sources, they should note all details of the source material rather than taking more generalized notes (A), and differentiate clearly not only between quotations and paraphrases (B), but also between their own paraphrases and their own commentaries (D). Essentially, they must clearly differentiate among direct quotations from sources, their own paraphrases of statements in sources, and their own commentaries on those source statements (C).

93. D: Teachers can much more easily diagnose specific reading difficulties in a few students at a time within a small group than in a whole class. Small-group instruction also makes it easier to design interventions for several students on similar reading levels with similar problem areas within a small group than for all students in a large class.

94. B: When using scaffolding, a teacher assigns a task that is just beyond the student's current level. The teacher encourages the student's attempts at comprehension by offering various supports that largely depend on prior knowledge, in order to develop the student's willingness to move forward into uncharted territory as a confident independent learner.

95. A: In the language experience approach, students decide on a story they want to tell and dictate it to a teacher, who writes the words down on paper. The teacher then reads the story back multiple times, modeling appropriate fluency. Students are then invited to join in reading the story. In writing workshop, students work on independent writing pieces following the stages of the writing process. They may all be involved in different stages at different times. Trait-based writing teaches students to consider the traits of good writing, such as word choice, throughout the writing process. During modeled writing, teachers think aloud as they record their thoughts on paper or on the board.

96. A: The gradual release model progresses in steps from explicit instruction to independent student work. First, in modeling and demonstration, students observe what the teacher does. Second, in teacher-led collaboration, students help what the teacher does. Third, in guided practice, students and teacher both do. Fourth, in student-led collaboration, the teacher helps what the students do. Fifth, in independent practice, the teacher observes and assesses what the students do.

97. D: Although there are many ready-made rubrics available online free of charge, and a teacher's selecting one this way eliminates added work (a), it does nothing to incorporate student input. Although the teacher knows the learning objectives and how to create a rubric, the teacher is not the only one who should do it (b): collaborating with students will not only ensure that they know and understand the learning objectives as well as teach them how to design rubrics, but it will also incorporate their input and feedback about curriculum and assessment into the design. Rather than collecting student input and then creating the rubric alone (c), the teacher should work together with all students to incorporate their input (d).

98. D: This description is most typical of the process of peer review. Classmates read Arthur's paper and then they identify values in it, describe it, ask questions about it, and suggest points for revision. These are types of helpful feedback identified by experts on writing and collaborative writing. The other choices, however, are not typically collaborative. For a portfolio assessment (A), the teacher collects finished work products from a student over time, eventually assembling a

Copyright © Mometrix Media. You have been licensed one copy of this document for personal use only. Any other reproduction or redistribution is strictly prohibited. All rights reserved. This content is provided for test preparation purposes only and does not imply an endorsement by Mometrix of any particular political, scientific, or religious point of view.

portfolio of work. This affords a more authentic assessment using richer, more multidimensional, and more visual and tactile products for assessment instead of using only standardized test scores for assessment. Holistic scoring (B) is a method of scoring a piece of writing for overall quality (evaluating general elements such as focus, organization, support, and conventions) rather than being overly concerned with any individual aspect of writing. A scoring rubric (C) is a guide that gives examples of the levels of typical characteristics in a piece of writing that correspond to each available score (for example, scores from 1-5).

99. D: Sending home leveled texts ensures that families have access to books in students' instructional reading levels. Providing the books allows students to read immediately and free of charge without requiring any trips to a library or bookstore. Choice A is also helpful, but without providing appropriate books, there is no guarantee that students will have access to reading materials. Notifying parents of which phonics skills the class practiced can also be helpful, but without providing additional information or materials, parents may not know how to best help their children practice these skills. Studying spelling words addresses the words in isolation rather than providing opportunities to read in context and practice decoding, comprehension, and fluency.

100. C: All private and public schools will provide some sort of curriculum guidance, which usually takes the form of a list of concepts that must be covered within a certain time frame. Teachers must use this provision as a guideline for planning instruction. However, with time and creativity, teachers can bring these concepts to life using various types of material (e.g., oral, written, media, and performance) and engaging instructional methods. Teachers can also find ways to integrate instruction and concepts with teachers of other subjects to ensure that students understand that language skills are not only interrelated, but also applicable to all areas of learning.

Integration of Knowledge and Understanding

101. Scoring Rubric:

Constructed response items will be scored holistically on a scale of 1-4 according to the following performance indicators:

Completion	The degree to which the candidate addresses all parts of the prompt
Organization/Clarity	The degree to which the candidate presents their response and supporting evidence in an organized, coherent manner
Accuracy/Relevancy	The degree to which the candidate demonstrates meaningful and accurate knowledge and skills pertaining to the prompt
Use of supporting evidence	The degree to which the candidate uses specific, appropriate, and relevant examples and reasoning from the exhibits provided

Candidates that receive an overall score of "4" demonstrate excellent pedagogical knowledge and skills related to the prompt.

- All parts of the prompt are addressed with thoroughness and attention to detail
- Information in the response is very well-organized, clear, and accessible to the reader
- The response demonstrates accurate and relevant pedagogical knowledge and skills relative to all items in the prompt
- The response includes ample specific, appropriate, and relevant examples from the exhibits provided with detailed explanations

Copyright © Mometrix Media. You have been licensed one copy of this document for personal use only. Any other reproduction or redistribution is strictly prohibited. All rights reserved. This content is provided for test preparation purposes only and does not imply an endorsement by Mometrix of any particular political, scientific, or religious point of view.

Practice Test #2

Multiple Choice Questions

1. Among specific components of reading difficulties, which category is a result of the other two?

    a. Difficulties with decoding words
    b. Difficulties with comprehending
    c. Difficulties with retention of text
    d. Difficulties with all are unrelated

2. A third-grade student has difficulties with decoding and struggles to read grade-level texts independently. Which statement is likely to be true based on this information?

    a. The student will benefit from additional implicit phonics instruction.
    b. The student will also struggle with phonological awareness.
    c. The student will also struggle with fluency and comprehension.
    d. The student likely has a language processing disorder and requires further evaluation.

3. What is true about speech or language delays and speech or language disorders?

    a. Delays and disorders both involve abnormal language development sequences.
    b. The only difference between delay and disorder is the severity of the problem.
    c. Speech or language disorders are more common than speech or language delays.
    d. Speech or language delays always involve slower language development rates.

4. What is the best way to utilize picture flashcards to develop children's phonemic awareness?

    a. The flashcards that are used should have pictures unfamiliar to the child.
    b. The child should be asked to identify a word's first and second phoneme.
    c. The child should be asked only to identify the word name of each picture.
    d. The flashcards should only be used for children with strong phonics skills.

5. What has research found about systematic, explicit instruction in phonics?

    a. It makes significant improvements in children's reading comprehension.
    b. It makes significant improvements in K-1 word recognition, not spelling.
    c. It makes significant improvements only for children with normal reading.
    d. It makes significant improvements as a whole beginner reading program.

6. What is one benefit of implicit phonics instruction?

    a. It leads to stronger decoding skills.
    b. Its progression from part to whole increases proficiency more quickly.
    c. Research suggests it is the most effective approach to phonics instruction.
    d. Phonics skills are taught in a meaningful context.

Copyright © Mometrix Media. You have been licensed one copy of this document for personal use only. Any other reproduction or redistribution is strictly prohibited. All rights reserved.
This content is provided for test preparation purposes only and does not imply an endorsement by Mometrix of any particular political, scientific, or religious point of view.

7. A teacher gives students a list of words, including *care, home,* and *use,* and asks them to record the definitions. Next, she asks them to add *less* to the ends of the words and record the new definitions. Students are then instructed to write down their observations in their writing journals. What is the primary purpose of this activity?

    a. Helping students recognize the meaning of a common suffix
    b. Teaching students the *-less* spelling pattern
    c. Practicing word analysis skills that will assist with decoding
    d. Identifying commonly used prefixes

8. A student can determine how to spell words like *psychology, psychiatrist, psychotic, psychopath, psychoactive,* etc., because they all start with the same Greek-derived prefix. This illustrates which type of spelling strategy?

    a. Morphemic spelling strategies
    b. Rule-based spelling strategies
    c. Phonetic spelling strategies
    d. Visual spelling strategies

9. Research shows that developmentally, which of these options is easiest for young children to identify?

    a. The medial and final phonemes of words
    b. The initial and medial phonemes of words
    c. Only the medial phonemes of words
    d. The initial and final phonemes of words

10. Regarding speech pre-production learning activities that teachers can use with ELL students to encourage them to speak English, which of the following is accurate?

    a. Choral readings afford advantages for beginning ELLs.
    b. Echo reading is not spontaneous and thus not useful.
    c. Shared reading and writing will not promote speech.
    d. Singing is vocal but otherwise irrelevant to speaking.

11. Students in a fifth-grade class are breaking the word *invisible* into its component parts. They identify the prefix *in-*, the root *vis*, and the suffix *-ible*, along with the meanings of each part. What type of activity is being demonstrated?

    a. Miscue analysis
    b. Structural analysis
    c. Syllabification
    d. Decoding

12. Which of these best identifies what developing automatic word recognition improves for students?

    a. Recall quality and organization, via fluency and comprehension
    b. Reading automaticity and speed, irrespective of comprehension
    c. Reading comprehension, irrespective of how reading is recalled
    d. Recall accuracy, organization, and detail irrespective of fluency

Copyright © Mometrix Media. You have been licensed one copy of this document for personal use only. Any other reproduction or redistribution is strictly prohibited. All rights reserved.
This content is provided for test preparation purposes only and does not imply an endorsement by Mometrix of any particular political, scientific, or religious point of view.

13. A kindergarten teacher notices that one of his students consistently understands and follows directions that are spoken to him. However, when he speaks in any situation, his sentences are often missing key words and don't make sense. The student is demonstrating difficulties with what?

- a. Expressive language
- b. Receptive language
- c. Pragmatic language
- d. Articulation

14. A kindergarten teacher pronounces a series of word pairs for her students. The students repeat the pairs. Some of the pairs rhyme (*see/bee*) and some of the pairs share initial sounds but do not rhyme (*sit, sun*). The students help her separate the word pairs into pairs that rhyme and pairs that do not. Once the students are able to distinguish between two words that rhyme and two words that do not, the teacher says a word and asks them to provide a rhyme. When she says *cat* a child responds with *fat*. When she says *sing* a child offers *thing*. How does this strictly oral activity contribute to the children's ability to read?

- a. It doesn't. Oral activities must have a written component to be useful to emergent readers.
- b. It is helpful in that it demonstrates how different sounds are made with different letters.
- c. It actually discourages children from reading. By emphasizing orality over literacy, the teacher is suggesting to the children that reading is not an important skill.
- d. Being able to identify rhyme is an important element of phonological awareness.

15. Which of these best reflects recommendations in instructional plans for teaching children the alphabetic principle?

- a. Practice opportunities with cumulative review and new relationships
- b. Explicitly teaching letter-sound correspondences in words to children
- c. Special weekly opportunities to practice letter-sound correspondence
- d. Opportunities to apply learning to unfamiliar, correctly spelled words

16. A teacher asks her students to say /ake/. She then tells students to add different consonant sounds to the beginning of /ake/ to see which real and nonsense words they can form. Which component of phonological awareness are students practicing in this activity?

- a. Syllabification
- b. Onsets and rimes
- c. Phoneme isolation
- d. Segmentation

17. Which of the following activities best demonstrates a phonics activity?

- a. Sorting rhyming words
- b. Playing alphabet bingo and covering a letter when the teacher says its name
- c. Matching picture cards to the consonant blends they begin with
- d. Listening to a fictional story read aloud by the teacher and identifying the setting

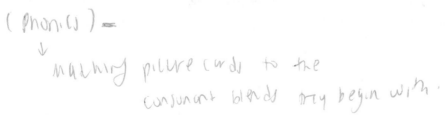

42

Copyright © Mometrix Media. You have been licensed one copy of this document for personal use only. Any other reproduction or redistribution is strictly prohibited. All rights reserved.
This content is provided for test preparation purposes only and does not imply an endorsement by Mometrix of any particular political, scientific, or religious point of view.

18. The most effective strategy for decoding sight words is:

a. Segmenting sight words into syllables. Beginning readers are understandably nervous when encountering a long word that isn't familiar. Blocking off all but a single syllable at a time renders a word manageable and allows the reader a sense of control over the act of reading.

b. Word families. By grouping the sight word with similar words, patterns emerge.

c. A phonemic approach. When students understand the connection between individual words and their sounds, they will be able to sound out any sight word they encounter.

d. None; sight words cannot be decoded. Readers must learn to recognize these as whole words on sight.

19. For students with problems retrieving or naming, which is the best instructional strategy to teach letter-sound associations?

a. Decoding closed-syllable, CVC words should begin after students master all consonant associations.

b. Decoding closed-syllable, CVC words should begin after students master all short vowel associations.

c. Decoding closed-syllable, CVC words should start after students master all consonants and one to two vowels.

d. Decoding closed-syllable, CVC words should begin once students master just a few of these associations.

20. Which of these is true about using music to teach sight words to kindergarten students?

a. Singing words to catchy tunes is a mnemonic device.

b. Singing is fun for children but does not aid memory.

c. Singing helps retain new words but not the spellings.

d. Singing is an activity that young children do not like.

21. Which of these is one of the signs that a student has difficulty with retaining reading?

a. The student's oral reading disregards punctuation.

b. The student's reading omits, or disregards, details.

c. The student's personal applying of content is poor.

d. The student's connection of text ideas is deficient.

22. Of the following, which is most correct related to children matching voice to print?

a. It is not normal for a second-grader to finger-point to words when reading.

b. Giving young children creative, fun pointers is wrong, as these are crutches.

c. Older student finger-pointing shows reading struggles and impedes fluency.

d. Using bookmarks/popsicle sticks sideways has no effect on finger-pointing.

23. Which choice represents a likely progression of phonological awareness skills?

a. Onset and rime manipulation, rhyming, phoneme deletion, syllabification

b. Phoneme deletion, syllabification, onset and rime manipulation, rhyming

c. Rhyming, syllabification, onset and rime manipulation, phoneme deletion

d. Syllabification, phoneme deletion, rhyming, onset and rime manipulation

A progression of Phonological Awareness skill

Rhyming

Syllabification

Onset and Rime Manipulation 43 Phoneme Deletion

Copyright © Mometrix Media. You have been licensed one copy of this document for personal use only. Any other reproduction or redistribution is strictly prohibited. All rights reserved.
This content is provided for test preparation purposes only and does not imply an endorsement by Mometrix of any particular political, scientific, or religious point of view.

24. Which statement best describes the relationship between phonological awareness and phonemic awareness?

    a.   Phonological awareness and phonemic awareness are interchangeable terms.

    b.   Phonological awareness is one specific component of phonemic awareness.

    c.   Phonemic awareness is one specific component of phonological awareness.

    d.   Phonological awareness typically develops after phonemic awareness.

25. Which of the following activities best demonstrates a multisensory approach to teaching letter formation?

    a.   Locating words containing a certain letter in a book

    b.   Tracing prewritten letters on paper with a pencil

    c.   Identifying letters on flashcards

    d.   Writing letters in shaving cream

26. Maria, a third-grade student, is reading a new chapter book for the first time. Her teacher observes as Maria struggles to decode the word *scapegoat* in the following sentence: "John frowned when he realized he was being made the scapegoat." Which of the following strategies would most likely assist Maria with decoding this word?

    a.   Using syntactic cues

    b.   Blending the sounds

    c.   Using context clues from the sentence

    d.   Chunking

27. A student is reading a fictional book and has difficulty decoding the word *maple*. Which spelling pattern could the teacher explain to help the student decode this word and similar words in the future?

    a.   Vowel digraph pairs

    b.   R-controlled vowels

    c.   Closed syllables

    d.   Open syllables

28. Which of the following options best demonstrates a kinesthetic activity to build sight word recognition?

    a.   Circling sight words found in a magazine article

    b.   Building sight words with letter tiles

    c.   Reading books containing numerous sight words

    d.   Hopping along sight words written in chalk

29. A kindergarten teacher says the words *tap* and *top* aloud. She asks students to identify whether the sound that is different is found in the beginning, middle, or ending of the words. Which skill does this activity practice?

    a.   Phoneme substitution

    b.   Phoneme discrimination

    c.   Phoneme deletion

    d.   Phoneme insertion

Copyright © Mometrix Media. You have been licensed one copy of this document for personal use only. Any other reproduction or redistribution is strictly prohibited. All rights reserved.
This content is provided for test preparation purposes only and does not imply an endorsement by Mometrix of any particular political, scientific, or religious point of view.

30. What is most accurate about the benefits of various levels of phonological awareness instruction to the development of reading skills?

    a. Instruction in rhyming and onsets and rimes appears most directly beneficial to reading development.

    b. Instruction in simpler phonology skills can aid teaching more complex ones and reading development.

    c. Instruction that integrates blending and segmenting appears most beneficial to reading development.

    d. Instruction that integrates deleting and substituting appears most beneficial to reading development.

31. A student incorrectly pronounces the word *rattle* with a long vowel *a*. The teacher explains a general rule to the student about splitting doubled consonants. This instructional strategy focuses most on using which of these?

    a. Structural analysis

    b. Spelling patterns

    c. Syllabication

    d. Morphemes

32. Which of the following is incorrect about teaching students the distinction between vowels as open sounds and consonants as closed sounds?

    a. This should be taught for the first time when teaching letter-sound matching.

    b. This should be introduced when initially teaching phonemic awareness.

    c. This should be reviewed after teaching some letter shapes and names.

    d. This should be reviewed after teaching some letter decoding.

33. In an oddity task to demonstrate student ability to identify words with the same and different initial, medial, and final phonemes in words, which of these asks students to identify words with the same medial consonant sound?

    a. Identifying *pan* and *cat* from among *pan, top,* and *cat*

    b. Identifying *lesson* and *missing* in *lesson, kitten, missing*

    c. Identifying *feet* as different among *late, feet,* and *take*

    d. Identifying *ten* and *man* from among *ten, sat,* and *man*

34. Students in a second-grade classroom are exploring and building words that contain *eigh*. Which layer of orthography are they exploring?

    a. Alphabet layer

    b. Pattern layer

    c. Meaning layer

    d. Conventional layer

Copyright © Mometrix Media. You have been licensed one copy of this document for personal use only. Any other reproduction or redistribution is strictly prohibited. All rights reserved. This content is provided for test preparation purposes only and does not imply an endorsement by Mometrix of any particular political, scientific, or religious point of view.

35. Researchers have identified five developmental stages of spelling. Which choice orders these stages in the correct sequence of development?

a. Derivational relations spelling, emergent spelling, letter name-alphabetic spelling, syllables and affixes spelling, within-word pattern spelling

b. Letter name-alphabetic spelling, syllables and affixes spelling, within-word pattern spelling, emergent spelling, derivational relations spelling

c. Emergent spelling, letter name-alphabetic spelling, within-word pattern spelling, syllables and affixes spelling, derivational relations spelling

d. Within-word pattern spelling, emergent spelling, derivational relations spelling, syllables and affixes spelling, letter name-alphabetic spelling

36. According to experts, which of the following is an accurate distinction regarding phonological awareness and phonemic awareness?

a. Phonological awareness distinguishes speech sounds from meanings.

b. There is no real distinction; they are synonyms used interchangeably.

c. Phonological awareness involves sounds, phonemic involves speech.

d. Phonemic awareness is the less sophisticated level between the two.

37. Among the following, which is NOT a common academic standard for kindergarten students in decoding and identifying words?

a. Showing knowledge that letter sequences correspond to phoneme sequences

b. Understanding that word sounds and meanings change along with word letters

c. Decoding monosyllabic words using initial and final consonant and vowel sounds

d. Matching letters to consonant sounds; reading simple, monosyllabic sight words

38. Concerning spelling, what statement is correct about how children learn?

a. Children must be taught spelling patterns as they will not learn them incidentally.

b. Children who know basic spelling rules can deduce spellings for words they hear.

c. Children may be able to spell words, but this does not mean they can read them.

d. Children's reading and writing skills promote spelling, but the reverse is not true.

39. According to research findings, which of these is an example of effective instructional practices to support English language acquisition for ELL students?

a. Encouraging independence by assigning projects only individually

b. Writing problems and directions in shorter and simpler sentences

c. Emphasizing how quickly students finish work, not how accurately

d. Asking only questions they can answer using lower level cognition

40. For supporting language acquisition in ESL/ELL students, what is most accurate about research-based instructional practices?

a. Teachers should only state directions verbally to give ELLs English decoding practice.

b. Teachers should encourage ESL students to respond rapidly to get them up to speed.

c. Teachers should use idioms without explanations to familiarize ELL students to these.

d. Teachers should give ELL students models and examples of what they expect in tasks.

Copyright © Mometrix Media. You have been licensed one copy of this document for personal use only. Any other reproduction or redistribution is strictly prohibited. All rights reserved.
This content is provided for test preparation purposes only and does not imply an endorsement by Mometrix of any particular political, scientific, or religious point of view.

41. Which of the following choices describes the best introduction to a unit on oral traditions from around the world?

    a. Introducing games that practice new sight words, encoding words based on phonics rules, and answering short comprehension questions.

    b. Setting up video-conferencing with a school in Asia so that students can communicate with children from other countries.

    c. Inviting a guest speaker from a nearby Native American group to demonstrate oral storytelling to the class.

    d. Creating a slide show presentation about various types of oral cultures and traditions and characteristics of each.

42. Homonyms such as *bare* and *bear* are similar in sound yet have different meanings. What would a teacher suggest a student do to avoid misusing these words?

    a. Memorize the definitions of the difficult words.

    b. Check a dictionary or thesaurus to verify a word's usage.

    c. Avoid encountering difficult words.

    d. Ignore being precise in the definition.

43. When a teacher instructs elementary school students in analyzing phonetically-regular words, which of the following would best represent a sequence from simpler to progressively more complex?

    a. Long vowels, short vowels, consonant blends, CVC (consonant-vowel-consonant) and other common patterns, individual phonemes, blending phonemes, types of syllables, onsets and rimes

    b. Onsets and rimes, short vowels, consonant blends, long vowels, blending phonemes, CVC and other common patterns, types of syllables, individual phonemes

    c. Types of syllables, onsets and rimes, CVC and other common patterns, consonant blends, blending phonemes, individual phonemes, long vowels, short vowels

    d. Individual phonemes, blending phonemes, onsets and rimes, short vowels, long vowels, consonant blends, CVC and other common patterns, types of syllables

44. A student learning English as a second language (ESL) who has limited comprehension of English and can speak one- to two-word English answers, essential English words, present-tense English verbs, and some familiar English phrases is in which stage of second-language acquisition?

    a. Preproduction

    b. Early Production

    c. Speech Emergence

    d. Intermediate Fluency

45. As one approach to gathering student input, what is correct about a K.I.M. chart for learning vocabulary?

    a. The K in K.I.M. stands for Know, the I for Identify, and the M for Meaning.

    b. Under the K in a K.I.M. chart, the student enters the definitions of the word.

    c. Under the K in a K.I.M. chart, the student enters the new vocabulary words.

    d. When students make K.I.M. charts, they never include drawings or pictures.

Copyright © Mometrix Media. You have been licensed one copy of this document for personal use only. Any other reproduction or redistribution is strictly prohibited. All rights reserved.
This content is provided for test preparation purposes only and does not imply an endorsement by Mometrix of any particular political, scientific, or religious point of view.

46. Collaborative Strategic Reading (CSR) is a teaching technique that depends on two teaching practices. These practices are:
  a. Cooperative learning and reading comprehension
  b. Cooperative reading and metacognition
  c. Reading comprehension and metacognition
  d. Cooperative learning and metacognition

47. A sixth-grade science teacher wants to help his students recognize connections between words containing the same Latin root. Which activity would most likely achieve this goal?
  a. Defining words containing the root using a dictionary
  b. Creating a semantic map
  c. Searching for words containing the root in the science textbook
  d. Comparing and contrasting words containing the root using a Venn diagram

48. Educational researchers have found which of the following literary genres most appropriate for improving reading comprehension in public schools?
  a. Novels
  b. Poems
  c. Short stories
  d. Drama (plays)

49. What is a valid guideline for teachers to follow in instructional activities that help students practice evaluating information sources?
  a. Practicing evaluation during ongoing discussion can engage students more deeply.
  b. Practicing evaluation should be reserved until after students have discussed topics.
  c. Teachers should provide long, complete passages from different topical resources.
  d. Students should evaluate material using unlimited numbers of open-ended questions.

50. Every year, a social studies teacher teaches her students a large variety of vocabulary words that are new to her students. She wants students to not only learn the definitions, but also have a deep understanding of the concept of the new words. Which of the following activities would work best with achieving this teacher's goal?
  a. When a new vocabulary word is introduced, assist students in creating word maps on the new words
  b. Make sure that each set of desks includes dictionaries so students are always able to look up the meanings of words they are unsure of
  c. Create a list on the wall of new topics so students know they are not expected to have learned them until this year
  d. When speaking in class, use the new vocabulary words as much as possible to ensure a deeper understanding

51. Which of these teaching/learning strategies associated with indirect instruction most promotes student visualization, organization, and application of ideas they have learned?
  a. Reading for meaning
  b. Concept mapping
  c. Cloze procedures
  d. Case studies

Copyright © Mometrix Media. You have been licensed one copy of this document for personal use only. Any other reproduction or redistribution is strictly prohibited. All rights reserved.
This content is provided for test preparation purposes only and does not imply an endorsement by Mometrix of any particular political, scientific, or religious point of view.

52. Which of the following questions requires students to make an inference about a fictional text?

    a. Did the author support her points with strong evidence?
    b. How do you think the character felt when she said that?
    c. What do you think will happen next?
    d. Does this character remind you of any characters in other books you have read?

53. Among principles of effective writing instruction, which of these reflects teaching discourse knowledge that enables more effective student writing?

    a. Varying levels of explicit instruction, using small groups, and varying amounts of writing instruction time
    b. Allowing sufficient time for systematic writing opportunities in both ELA classes and all content subjects
    c. Incorporating reasons and methods for explicit writing instruction, including feedback and collaboration
    d. Organizing writing effectively for various subjects, plus spelling, vocabulary, syntax, etc., for the subjects

54. When can making a KWL chart help students with reading comprehension?

    a. Before, during, and after students read
    b. Before and during but not after reading
    c. During and after but not before reading
    d. Before and after but not during reading

55. The use of analogies is most appropriate for helping students achieve which instructional objective?

    a. Analyzing common roots and affixes
    b. Defining words
    c. Identifying word origins
    d. Recognizing the relationships between words

56. Before asking students to read a new fiction book independently, the teacher conducts a picture walk with the class. What is the teacher's primary goal for conducting the picture walk?

    a. Encouraging the use of syntactic cues
    b. Setting a purpose for reading
    c. Activating students' prior knowledge
    d. Developing students' metacognitive skills

Copyright © Mometrix Media. You have been licensed one copy of this document for personal use only. Any other reproduction or redistribution is strictly prohibited. All rights reserved.
This content is provided for test preparation purposes only and does not imply an endorsement by Mometrix of any particular political, scientific, or religious point of view.

57. A third-grade science teacher gives her students one hour to read an article about penguins, take notes on important information, and use the notes to write a three-paragraph expository essay. At the end of the hour, Joshua only has his notes completed. The teacher examines his notes, part of which are shown below.

> Penguins are animals that live in the Southern Hemisphere.
>
> Many people believe that penguins live in the Arctic, but that is not true.
>
> Penguins in Antarctica huddle together to stay warm. They take turns standing on the outside of the huddle, where it is colder.
>
> Penguins' feathers help protect them from the water and cold air.
>
> Penguins live in groups called colonies.

Which strategy would be most helpful for the teacher to focus on with Joshua to prepare him for similar tasks?

   a. Grouping the notes into three sections to correspond with the paragraphs of the essay
   b. Selecting only a few facts to record before moving on to the essay
   c. Using drawings rather than words
   d. Recording only key words and phrases rather than sentences

58. Using E. B. White's *Stuart Little* as an example, which response represents evaluative comprehension?

   a. "Stuart Little, who is the main character in this story, is a mouse."
   b. "Stuart's parents, Mr. and Mrs. Frederick C. Little, are humans."
   c. "Stuart's size and doing things a mouse can do help his family."
   d. "Stuart likes to be first up in the morning; I like to sleep late." *Text to self connection*

59. In writing instruction, which of these correctly represents some of the things that teachers should instruct students to consider about the audience for whom they will be writing?

   a. They must consider who will read it, but the format (oral presentation, blog, school newspaper, etc.) is irrelevant.
   b. They must consider reading level(s), vocabulary, and writing length the audience expects more than the message.
   c. They must consider the message they want to convey more than the format in which the audience will receive it.
   d. They must consider the type of writing that their intended audience will expect as much as who that audience is.

60. Which of the following options best demonstrates a specific and measurable reading intervention goal for a first grader?

   a. The student will increase his score on the DIBELS Nonsense Word Fluency: Whole Words Read assessment from 10 to 15 by May 30 of this year.
   b. The student will read at a DRA level 14.
   c. The student will increase his oral reading rate on the DIBELS: Oral Reading Fluency assessment by December 15 of this year.
   d. The student will meet grade-level benchmarks on the DRA.

Copyright © Mometrix Media. You have been licensed one copy of this document for personal use only. Any other reproduction or redistribution is strictly prohibited. All rights reserved.
This content is provided for test preparation purposes only and does not imply an endorsement by Mometrix of any particular political, scientific, or religious point of view.

61. Which of these is mainly a sign that a student has problems with reading comprehension?

    a.   The student has trouble recognizing words out of context.

    b.   The student reads laboriously, reading one word at a time.

    c.   The student has trouble separating the main idea from details.

    d.   The student has trouble relating a text to prior knowledge.

62. Practical instructional activities that develop student listening skills include which of these?

    a.   Teaching students how to follow rather than give directions

    b.   Teaching students how to give rather than follow directions

    c.   Teaching students the skills of interpersonal communication

    d.   Teaching students to appreciate conversation, not literature

63. Mr. Suarez teaches a preschool class containing students in the preliterate stage of writing. He wants to help his students understand the relationship between spoken and written words using a familiar topic, so he has planned an activity relating to the class's recent field trip to the apple orchard. The group will record memories of their field trip in writing, and Mr. Suarez will read the writing back to students repeatedly throughout the week. Which activity would be most appropriate?

    a.   Shared writing

    b.   Independent writing

    c.   Interactive writing

    d.   Partner writing

64. Students in a sixth-grade classroom are reading a persuasive essay about the importance of recycling. Which question can the teacher ask to help students develop evaluative comprehension skills?

    a.   Do you agree with the author that recycling is an easy way for everyone to help the environment?

    b.   Which material takes longer to decompose: plastic or glass?

    c.   What types of materials can be recycled?

    d.   Who should you contact in your city if you want to help organize a recycling program?

65. Which instructional strategy is most closely related to and is a key component of schema theory?

    a.   Summarizing

    b.   Activating prior knowledge

    c.   Identifying main idea

    d.   Recognizing story elements

66. To help students find and use evidence from nonfictional text to support their ideas, which instructional strategy is most applicable?

    a.   Inquiry Charts (I-Charts)

    b.   Graphic organizers

    c.   Journaling

    d.   RAFT

Copyright © Mometrix Media. You have been licensed one copy of this document for personal use only. Any other reproduction or redistribution is strictly prohibited. All rights reserved. This content is provided for test preparation purposes only and does not imply an endorsement by Mometrix of any particular political, scientific, or religious point of view.

67. William, a third-grade student, recently wrote, "The cars drives down the street," in his writing journal. His teacher notices that he makes similar errors in other sentences he writes. He also makes these types of errors when reading. For example, he recently said, "The birds flies in the sky," while reading a text. Which grammatical skill should the teacher work on with William?

   a. Pronoun-antecedent agreement
   b. Consistent verb tenses
   c. Subject-verb agreement
   d. Complex sentences

68. A teacher wants to introduce the concept of connotative and denotative meanings while reading a novel. He plans to use character traits as a way to introduce this topic. Which set of words to describe a character would best help him introduce and explain connotative and denotative word meanings?

   a. Kind and nice
   b. Happy and joyful
   c. Determined and persistent
   d. Frugal and cheap

69. Which instructional strategy would be most appropriate to assist a student with retention difficulties in analyzing the plot of a fictional text?

   a. Providing the student with a story map
   b. Having the student read the story twice before responding to questions
   c. Playing an audio version of the story rather than having the student read a printed version
   d. Asking the student to compete a KWL chart before and after reading

70. Among instructional strategies to aid student comprehension of nonfictional text, which of these is most useful for promoting critical thinking?

   a. Answering open-ended questions about texts
   b. Skimming the text for features that give signs
   c. Establishing connections between text and life
   d. Establishing connections between text and self

71. Among reading materials teachers can select to promote student comprehension of nonfiction, most content-area textbooks used in public schools feature which type of writing?

   a. Narrative
   b. Persuasive
   c. Descriptive
   d. Informational

72. Of the following, which represents an indirect way in which students receive instruction in and learn vocabulary?

   a. Being exposed repeatedly to vocabulary in multiple teaching contexts
   b. Being exposed to vocabulary when adults read aloud to them
   c. Being pre-taught specific words found in text prior to reading
   d. Being taught vocabulary words over extended periods of time

Copyright © Mometrix Media. You have been licensed one copy of this document for personal use only. Any other reproduction or redistribution is strictly prohibited. All rights reserved. This content is provided for test preparation purposes only and does not imply an endorsement by Mometrix of any particular political, scientific, or religious point of view.

73. Young children are more likely to respond to analogies in stories rather than to metaphors because:

    a. They are old enough to understand the abstract thinking and symbolism that analogies express.

    b. The ability to understand the kinds of abstraction expressed in metaphors is not developed until later in childhood.

    c. They can apply the concepts expressed in analogies to their own daily lives, but metaphors do not compare things that children are familiar with.

    d. Metaphors and symbols are usually found only in books that children find boring because of their abstractions.

74. Which of the following is the most effective way for a first-grade teacher to enhance students' reading proficiency?

    a. Provide effective phonics instruction

    b. Encourage oral storytelling in the classroom

    c. Replace basal texts with real literature

    d. Have students make daily visits to the school library

75. Teachers must consider student developmental levels when assigning cooperative learning projects and/or discussions. For example, students are bored by topics at younger age levels and lost by topics at older ones. In addition to chronological age, which other developmental level does this example relate to most?

    a. Social developmental levels

    b. Cognitive developmental levels

    c. Emotional developmental levels

    d. Behavioral developmental levels

76. To provide accommodations for ELL students, which of these should teachers do in vocabulary and reading instruction?

    a. Teach ELL students vocabulary in isolation.

    b. Teach ELL students vocabulary in context.

    c. Teach ELL students vocabulary in volume.

    d. Teach ELL students reading by their speech levels.

77. Which of the following methods would give students the most *objective* feedback to enable them to monitor their own performance and progress in speaking and enacting through giving oral reports and presentations?

    a. Having classmates offer peer reviews

    b. Having a teacher evaluate their work

    c. Comparing their work to classmates' work

    d. Viewing videos of their performance

Copyright © Mometrix Media. You have been licensed one copy of this document for personal use only. Any other reproduction or redistribution is strictly prohibited. All rights reserved. This content is provided for test preparation purposes only and does not imply an endorsement by Mometrix of any particular political, scientific, or religious point of view.

78. In a paired reading strategy for identifying the main idea in informational text, two students silently read a selection. Then, taking two-column notes of main ideas and supporting details, they take turns with the following steps. Which choice sequences these steps in the correct order?

   a. The pair develops main idea consensus, a student paraphrases the main idea, a student explains agreement or disagreement, they take turns finding supporting details
   b. A student paraphrases the main idea, a student explains agreement or disagreement, the pair develops main idea consensus, they take turns finding supporting details
   c. They take turns finding supporting details, a student explains agreement or disagreement, a student paraphrases the main idea, the pair develops main idea consensus
   d. A student explains agreement or disagreement, they take turns finding supporting details, the pair develops main idea consensus, a student paraphrases the main idea

79. During a reading assessment, which of the following student behaviors reflects a weakness in strategy?

   a. The student tries to read every word, with many errors.
   b. The student pays attention to the punctuation in a text.
   c. The student understands the main idea, but not details.
   d. The student takes a holistic approach to reading words.

80. Sixth-grade students are taking a standardized, criterion-referenced reading test. Part of the test involves answering comprehension questions based on reading passages. Some of the passages contain cultural references that some groups of students do not understand, causing them to miss multiple questions. This is an example of a testing concern in which area?

   a. Validity
   b. Reliability
   c. Bias
   d. Consistency

81. Which of the following is important when using performance-based assessments of student literacy?

   a. Establishing valid norms for student scoring
   b. Establishing clear, equitable scoring criteria
   c. Establishing single correct answers for items
   d. Establishing standard answer keys for scores

82. In a rubric for scoring oral English language proficiency in English language learners (ELLs), which of these would most reflect a criterion at the highest proficiency level?

   a. Being able to repeat English words and phrases
   b. Being able to name concrete objects upon sight
   c. Being able to participate in classroom discussions
   d. Being able to communicate well in social contexts

Copyright © Mometrix Media. You have been licensed one copy of this document for personal use only. Any other reproduction or redistribution is strictly prohibited. All rights reserved.
This content is provided for test preparation purposes only and does not imply an endorsement by Mometrix of any particular political, scientific, or religious point of view.

83. A teacher conducts an informal one-to-one reading assessment of rhyme recognition with a young child. Which of the following should the teacher always do first?

a. Ask the child whether he or she knows what rhyming words are.
b. Ask the child to demonstrate by saying two rhyming words.
c. Give the child an explanation by defining what rhymes are.
d. Give the child an example of a pair of words that rhyme.

84. A sentence in a book states, "They had several chores to do." Which of the following examples demonstrates a visual error, if stated by a student reading the text?

a. They had several jobs to do.
b. They had seven chores to do.
c. They had chores to do.
d. They had many chores to do.

85. Which of the following statements is true regarding screening and diagnostic assessments?

a. Screening assessments provide more thorough information than diagnostic assessments about students' specific strengths and needs.
b. Screening assessments are typically used to confirm diagnostic assessment results.
c. Screening assessments are used to identify students who may be at future risk of academic difficulties and may benefit from interventions.
d. Diagnostic assessments are used to identify students who may be at future risk of academic difficulties and may benefit from interventions.

86. Olivia, a first-grade student, has a reading intervention plan to improve her decoding of CVCe words. In addition to working with the teacher in a small group each day, Olivia's teacher gives her 10 new CVCe words to decode each Friday. The number of words read correctly is recorded on a graph, and the teacher notes any improvement made from the previous weeks. Which type of assessment is the teacher demonstrating?

a. Progress monitoring
b. Screening assessment
c. Summative assessment
d. Norm-referenced assessment

87. A sentence in a book states, "The furry dog chases the stick." Which of the following examples demonstrates a structural error, if stated by a student reading the text?

a. The furry dog chases the branch.
b. The furry dog chases the big stick.
c. The fuzzy dog chases the stick.
d. The furry dog chased the stick.

Copyright © Mometrix Media. You have been licensed one copy of this document for personal use only. Any other reproduction or redistribution is strictly prohibited. All rights reserved.
This content is provided for test preparation purposes only and does not imply an endorsement by Mometrix of any particular political, scientific, or religious point of view.

88. A second-grade teacher is planning a lesson on adjectives and will ask students to locate 10 adjectives in a text. Which modified activity would be the most appropriate way for the teacher to engage advanced students in exploring adjectives?

a. Asking them to locate 20 adjectives in the text
b. Asking students to locate vague adjectives in the text and then replace them with more specific adjectives
c. Pairing the proficient readers with struggling readers to complete the activity
d. Assigning the students an additional practice paper to complete after finding the 10 adjectives

89. Which of the following examples demonstrate students using a combination of digital and print-based media?

a. Students put sentence strips in order to retell the main events of a story they read in their reading textbook.
b. Students watch an animated story on an educational website and complete the accompanying online comprehension questions.
c. Students listen as their teacher reads a big book on plants aloud. Then they create a computer slideshow showing the stages of plant growth.
d. Students use free software to create a digital storyboard. Then they film a movie using the storyboard as a guide.

90. What have research studies found about computer-assisted instruction (CAI) programs for teaching reading and communication skills to students with various disabilities?

a. These programs increase reading skills but decrease interaction.
b. Multimedia software plus scaffolding teach this population less.
c. CAI with the Nonverbal Reading Approach was the most useful.
d. Student differences make individualizing instruction paramount.

Refer to the following for question 91:

> A reading teacher is working with a student who has just moved to Texas from Korea. The child knows very few words in English. The teacher offers her a picture book of Korean folk tales. Using words and gestures, the teacher asks her to "read" one folk tale. The child "reads" the familiar tale in Korean. The teacher then writes key English words on the board and asks the child to find those words in the book. When the child finds the words, they read them together.

91. The strategy used in this situation is:

a. Useful. The child will feel more confident because the story is already familiar. She will also feel that the lesson is a conversation of sorts, and that she is communicating successfully. She will be motivated to learn the English words because they are meaningful and highly charged.
b. Useful. The teacher is learning as much as the child is. The teacher is learning about Korean culture and language, and she can apply this knowledge when teaching future Korean students.
c. Not very useful. The child needs to be exposed to as much American culture as possible. Encouraging her to remember her own culture will make her sad and will limit her curiosity about her new home.
d. Not very useful. The first things the child should learn are the letters of the alphabet and associative sounds. Only then can she begin to decipher an unfamiliar language.

Copyright © Mometrix Media. You have been licensed one copy of this document for personal use only. Any other reproduction or redistribution is strictly prohibited. All rights reserved. This content is provided for test preparation purposes only and does not imply an endorsement by Mometrix of any particular political, scientific, or religious point of view.

92. A teacher uses a mixture of whole-group and small-group reading instruction. Which of the following activities would be the best choice for a whole-group lesson rather than small-group or individualized instruction?

a. Practice applying specific phonics skills
b. Independent reading of unfamiliar texts
c. Analyzing character development after the teacher reads a novel aloud
d. Spelling patterns

93. In investigating the best instructional strategies and tools for planning and implementing school reading programs, what have researchers found?

a. Explicit phonics instruction enables higher achievement only for at-risk students.
b. Instruction incorporating decodable books has been discredited by researchers.
c. Student use of word identification strategies is unrelated to what text they read.
d. Prior student literacy knowledge helps to develop sound-spelling understanding.

94. Some teachers have integrated smartphones into school curriculum as a way of using available technology to support the learning and practice of student research. What is correct about this trend?

a. Smartphones are projected to become too expensive as teaching tools.
b. Teachers should allow students to use the smartphones that they have.
c. It is unnecessary for a school to create an acceptable use policy for this.
d. Teachers need not know how to get information from students' phones.

95. Which of these best describes characteristics of K-12 curriculum designs for reading?

a. Designing a K-12 reading curriculum requires following a series of steps in rigid order.
b. Regardless of systematic planning and inventive thinking, compromises are inevitable.
c. Curriculum design decisions made at separate stages are independent of one another.
d. Conceptualizing curriculum design precedes specifications, development, and refinement.

96. Four central components of reading instruction reflect various learning opportunities in comprehensive literacy programs. According to the LEAD21 program, what are these components?

a. Whole-class reading, small-group reading, paired reading, and individual reading done by the students
b. Reading to students, with large student groups, with small student groups, and reading by the student
c. Interactive and community reading or read-alouds, differentiated reading, guided reading, and independent reading
d. Heterogeneous group reading, homogeneous group reading, reading partnerships, individual reading

97. In LEAD21 reading instruction, which of these factors are differentiated?

a. Teacher expectations and student tasks
b. Text choices and teacher support levels
c. Teacher expectations and support levels
d. Text choices and student tasks assigned

Copyright © Mometrix Media. You have been licensed one copy of this document for personal use only. Any other reproduction or redistribution is strictly prohibited. All rights reserved. This content is provided for test preparation purposes only and does not imply an endorsement by Mometrix of any particular political, scientific, or religious point of view.

98. Which of these is more characteristic of a summative assessment?
a. The teacher administers it frequently during instruction.
b. The teacher uses its results to inform teaching changes.
c. The teacher gives it after lessons, units, or school years are complete.
d. The teacher relies on it for individualizing student data.

99. Among assessments, which of these is typical of formative ones?
a. They are most often criterion-referenced tests.
b. They are most frequently norm-referenced tests.
c. They are most frequently standardized measures.
d. They are most often the most objective measures.

100. Which of the following is true about how teachers should use formal and informal instruments for formative assessment in the classroom?
a. Teachers should use multiple formal and informal assessments as bases for student grouping.
b. Teachers should use only formal test instruments for conducting their formative assessments.
c. Teachers should select one specific formal or informal assessment instrument to use exclusively.
d. Teachers should use formative assessments only for evaluating students, not for teaching them.

Copyright © Mometrix Media. You have been licensed one copy of this document for personal use only. Any other reproduction or redistribution is strictly prohibited. All rights reserved.
This content is provided for test preparation purposes only and does not imply an endorsement by Mometrix of any particular political, scientific, or religious point of view.

Answer Key and Explanations

Multiple Choice Questions

1. C: Difficulties with decoding words (A) involve problems separating written or printed words into the phonemes their letters represent and hearing and differentiating them. Many experts regard decoding difficulty as the source of most reading problems. Comprehension difficulties (B) result from decoding difficulties (A). Retention difficulties (C) result from difficulties with both comprehension (B) and decoding (A). Thus choice D is incorrect.

2. C: Decoding, fluency, and comprehension are interrelated. The student is likely spending a lot of mental energy trying to decode unknown words, leaving little energy left to focus on comprehension. Additionally, repeatedly stopping to decode words interrupts fluency. This may cause the reader to struggle to make connections between the disjointed words and sentences. Implicit phonics instruction is not the best intervention option, as research has shown that systematic and explicit phonics instruction is most effective. Additionally, there is not enough information available to determine the cause of the student's decoding difficulties. Therefore, it cannot be assumed that it is related to a lack of phonological awareness skills or a language processing disorder.

3. D: Speech or language delays involve a normal sequence of language development (A), but at slower rates (D) than normal, whereas speech or language disorders involve abnormal language development, including not following the normal sequence. Thus, severity is not the only difference (B). Speech or language delays are more common than speech or language disorders, not vice versa (C). In fact, speech or language delays are the most common developmental issue, affecting 5-10 percent of preschoolers.

4. B: When creating picture flashcards to help teach children phonemic awareness, the pictures chosen should be familiar to the child (A) so he or she can name them. The child should be asked not only to name each picture with a word (C), but also, after naming it, to identify the first and second phonemes in the word (B). This helps the child understand that words contain individual sounds. This strategy is particularly helpful for children who do not have strong phonics skills (D), which involve sound-letter correspondences.

5. A: Literacy research funded by the US Department of Education finds that systematic, explicit phonics instruction significantly improves children's reading comprehension, as well as both word recognition and spelling (B), and is especially effective for children having trouble learning to read (C). It does not, however, constitute a whole reading program for beginners (D), which includes alphabet knowledge, phonemic awareness, listening to read-alouds, reading aloud and silently, and writing letters, words, sentences, paragraphs, and stories in addition to phonics instruction.

6. D: Implicit phonics instruction uses a whole-to-part approach, with students reading whole texts rather than starting with isolated phonemes. Students learn to recognize whole words by sight. Through analyzing and comparing words, they then discover phonics and spelling patterns. A benefit is that students read authentic texts and learn in a meaningful context rather than practicing skills in isolation. However, research has shown that explicit phonics instruction, which progresses from part to whole, leads to stronger decoding, spelling, and comprehension skills.

7. A: The focus of this activity is on comparing the meanings of the words before and after the suffix *less* is added. Students should recognize that the newly formed words mean *without* (base word)

59

Copyright © Mometrix Media. You have been licensed one copy of this document for personal use only. Any other reproduction or redistribution is strictly prohibited. All rights reserved. This content is provided for test preparation purposes only and does not imply an endorsement by Mometrix of any particular political, scientific, or religious point of view.

and be able to apply this knowledge to figure out the meanings of other words containing the same suffix. While students may also learn to spell and decode words containing *less* as a result of this activity, the primary focus is on the words' meanings. Choice D is incorrect because *less* is a suffix. Prefixes are letters or groups of letters added to the beginnings of words.

8. A: Morphemic spelling strategies are based on how meaning influences spelling. Students learn these through learning Greek, Latin, and other root and affix derivations, adding affixes to roots, and forming abbreviations and compound words. Rule-based spelling strategies (B) include knowing that multiple spellings can exist for one phoneme, vowel and consonant interactions, and other generalizations. Phonetic spelling strategies (C), which are the easiest and should be taught first, identify a (regular) word's individual phonemes and spell it using the corresponding letters. Visual spelling strategies (D) use visual memory of spelling concepts: correct spellings look right.

9. D: Research (cf. Inverizzi, 2003) shows that in the normal developmental sequence of phonemic awareness abilities, it is much easier for young children to identify initial phonemes (at the beginnings of words) and final phonemes (at the ends of words) than it is for them to identify medial phonemes (in the middles of words). This demonstrates the importance of systematic instruction.

10. A: Teachers can encourage ELLs to speak English through meaningful activities that include choral readings, which are less daunting than solo readings, give a sense of safety and strength in numbers, and provide the least proficient or confident students with multiple models or partners. Echo reading is useful (B) by modeling correct reading that students emulate. Shared reading and writing promote both understanding and use of English language, thus promoting English speech (C). Singing encourages speech (D) by providing an easier way to vocalize in English through the added structure of melody and rhythm and the ability to memorize lyrics beforehand.

11. B: Students are analyzing the structure of the word by identifying the prefix, root, and suffix. Miscue analysis refers to analyzing reading errors to determine patterns in the strategies that students are using. Syllabification refers to breaking words into syllables. Because the suffix *-ible* has two syllables, and students are focusing on the meanings of the word parts, they are not focused on syllabification. Decoding is the process of translating graphemes into phonemes, or letters into sounds. In this example, students are focusing on identifying the word parts and their meanings rather than on simply decoding and reading the word.

12. A: The more words a student can recognize automatically when reading, the more fluently he or she reads, with better comprehension; these in turn dramatically enhance the student's ability to recall the reading more accurately, with greater organization and detail. Fluency without understanding (B), understanding without fluency (C), and improved recall without or regardless of fluency (D) are hence incorrect.

13. A: The student is demonstrating difficulties with expressive language, or ability to use spoken language to communicate as expected. Because he appears to understand and respond appropriately to speech he has heard, he is not displaying any difficulties with receptive language. Pragmatic language involves using language in ways that are appropriate for specific social situations. Because the student's difficulties are occurring in all contexts, they appear to be more related to expressive language than pragmatics. Articulation refers to difficulties making certain sounds. For example, sounds may be added or omitted from individual words. However, the student in this example is omitting entire words.

Copyright © Mometrix Media. You have been licensed one copy of this document for personal use only. Any other reproduction or redistribution is strictly prohibited. All rights reserved. This content is provided for test preparation purposes only and does not imply an endorsement by Mometrix of any particular political, scientific, or religious point of view.

14. D: Young children use language in a solely oral way. Oral language is composed of separate sounds that are represented in written form by the alphabet. In order to read, a child must first have a sense of the sounds that are used in English (phonological awareness). By helping children hear the difference between rhyming and non-rhyming words, the teacher is preparing them to make the transition to sound–letter association and word families.

15. A: Experts recommend that instructional plans for teaching the alphabetic principle include practice opportunities for both new letter-sound relationships and cumulative reviews of relationships taught earlier; teaching letter-sound correspondences to children explicitly, and in isolation, not in words (B); giving children opportunities to practice these correspondences during daily lessons (C); and giving them opportunities to apply their progressive learning of these correspondences to reading familiar, phonetically spelled words (D).

16. B: When students combine the initial sound in a word with the remainder of the word, they are blending the onset and rime. Syllabification involves breaking a word into syllables. A word may have one or more syllables. Phoneme isolation involves identifying either the beginning, middle, or ending sound in a word. Segmentation involves breaking a word into its individual sounds.

17. C: When students match picture cards with the consonant blends they begin with, they are using their understanding of the relationships between letters and the sounds they make. Therefore, it is a phonics activity. Choice A is a phonological awareness activity because it deals with sounds rather than letter/sound relationships. Choice B is a letter identification activity because students are matching letters to their names without addressing the sounds they make. Choice D is a comprehension activity because students are listening to a story and identifying story elements. They are not decoding the text independently.

18. D: None; sight words cannot be decoded. Readers must learn to recognize these as whole words on sight. Sight words have irregular spelling. Segmenting them into syllables or using a phonemic approach are ineffective strategies to aid a reader in recognizing a sight word because these approaches depend on rules a sight word doesn't follow. Word families group words that share common patterns of consonants and vowels. The spelling of those words is, therefore, regular because they follow a predictable pattern. Sight words are irregular, do not follow a predictable pattern, and must be instantaneously recognized for writing fluency. No decoding is useful.

19. D: It is not necessary for students with retrieving or naming problems to master all consonant letter-sound associations (A) or all short vowel letter-sound associations (B) to begin decoding closed-syllable words with the consonant-vowel-consonant (CVC) pattern, or to master all consonant and one to two vowel (C) associations. Once they have mastered one to two *short* vowel sound-letter associations, like [a] and [i], and several high-frequency consonant sound-letter associations (D), like [t], [b], [s], [f], and [m], teachers can start this decoding instruction, also gradually adding more letter-sound associations and reviewing often.

20. A: When kindergarten teachers lead children in singing sight words to catchy tunes, the association of words with music is a mnemonic device that is fun and helps them remember (B) both new words and how to spell them (C). Young children generally love singing (D), making this activity entertaining as well as effective for them to learn sight words.

21. C: If a student reads aloud without any vocal changes to identify text punctuation (A), this is a sign of difficulty with decoding words. Leaving out or glossing over or minimizing details (B) in reading text is one of the signs of difficulty with reading comprehension. Having problems applying

Copyright © Mometrix Media. You have been licensed one copy of this document for personal use only. Any other reproduction or redistribution is strictly prohibited. All rights reserved.
This content is provided for test preparation purposes only and does not imply an endorsement by Mometrix of any particular political, scientific, or religious point of view.

reading content to his or her own personal life (C) and connecting ideas (D) within a text passage are both among the signs of difficulty with reading retention.

22. C: Finger-pointing is normal for beginning readers, even into second grade (A); adults should not interfere with pointing. Giving young children "witch fingers," feathers, and other available, recycled, or homemade pointers is fine; these are not crutches (B), simply finger substitutes that are creative, fun, and keep book pages clean with younger readers. However, when older students finger-point, it can indicate reading struggles and interfere with reading fluency (C). Having students turn bookmarks or popsicle sticks sideways to mark each line of text helps them transition past finger-pointing (D).

23. C: Phonological awareness skills typically progress in a similar manner. The ability to rhyme often develops first, as it is considered the simplest skill. Later, children develop the ability to break words into syllables, which is usually followed by the ability to manipulate onsets and rimes. Phoneme isolation and other phonemic awareness skills typically develop last, as they are the most complex.

24. C: Phonological awareness and phonemic awareness are distinct terms. Phonological awareness is a broader term that refers to the ability to identify and manipulate sounds in spoken words. Phonemic awareness is one component of phonological awareness involving the ability to identify and manipulate sounds in spoken words at the phoneme level. Because phonemes are the smallest units of speech, phonemic awareness is an advanced component of phonological awareness. It typically develops after simpler skills, like rhyming and blending.

25. D: While all of these options can assist students with learning letter formation, writing letters in shaving cream best represents a multisensory approach. It involves movement, touch, and sight.

26. D: Chunking involves looking for known parts in a word. Because *scapegoat* is a compound word, it is likely that Maria will at least recognize the word *goat*. This leaves a smaller portion of the word to decode. There are many words that would sound right in the sentence, so guessing based on syntax alone is unlikely to result in the correct word. Because the word is multisyllabic and contains multiple spelling patterns, blending may be difficult. Additionally, the sentence provides few context clues to help Maria guess the word correctly.

27. D: The word *maple* begins with an open syllable, spelled *ma*. Open syllables end with a vowel and usually have a long vowel sound. Knowing this will help the student decode this word and other words with open syllables. This word does not contain any vowel digraph pairs, r-controlled vowels, or closed syllables. Vowel digraph pairs consist of two vowels that together make one sound. R-controlled vowels consist of a vowel before the letter *r*. Closed syllables end with a consonant and usually have a short vowel sound.

28. D: When students participate in kinesthetic activities, they are physically engaged in the learning process. These activities involve movement, such as hopping along the sight words written in chalk. While the other activities can also be used to practice sight words and may involve tactile experiences, they involve less movement and physical activity than hopping.

29. B: In this activity, students are identifying the discriminating phoneme in two words. In the example of *tap* and *top*, it is the middle phoneme that is different. To practice phoneme substitution, the teacher would give students a word and then instruct them to change one of the phonemes and identify the newly formed word. In phoneme deletion, the teacher would give students a word and instruct them to remove a phoneme and identify the newly formed word. In phoneme insertion, the

Copyright © Mometrix Media. You have been licensed one copy of this document for personal use only. Any other reproduction or redistribution is strictly prohibited. All rights reserved. This content is provided for test preparation purposes only and does not imply an endorsement by Mometrix of any particular political, scientific, or religious point of view.

teacher would give students a word and instruct them to add a phoneme and identify the newly formed word.

30. C: Researchers have found that instruction in simpler phonological skills like rhyming and onsets and rimes may not have any direct benefits for reading development (A); however, they find that teaching these simpler skills first nevertheless can make it easier to teach the more complex ones *without* directly benefiting reading development (B). Researchers have also found that the phonological awareness instruction that appears most beneficial to subsequent reading development integrates blending and segmenting (C), not deleting and substituting (D).

31. C: The general rule about splitting doubled consonants pertains most to syllabication, i.e., where to divide words up into their component syllables to inform pronunciation and meaning. Structural analysis (A) pertains to dividing words into component parts like prefixes, roots, and suffixes, which may or may not coincide with syllable divisions. Using common spelling patterns (B) pertains to determining meaning and pronunciation in unfamiliar words by comparing their spelling to the same or similar spellings in familiar words. Using morphemes (D) pertains to identifying the smallest meaningful grammatical units in words, e.g., *-ed* verb endings signify past tense.

32. A: The distinction between vowel and consonant sounds should not be taught for the first time when teaching which letters represent which sounds, but introduced earlier, during instruction in phonemic awareness. This concept should be reviewed after teaching students to decode a small set of letter-sound matches and to recognize and form letter shapes and names.

33. B: Both words identified in this choice have the same medial consonant sound of /s/, whereas *kitten* has the medial consonant /t/. The two words identified in choice A have the same medial *vowel* sound. The one word identified in choice C has a different medial *vowel* sound than the other two. The two words identified in choice D have the same *final* consonant sound; the other word does not.

34. B: The pattern layer of orthography involves looking at groups of letters within words that form patterns. Therefore, exploring and building words that all contain *eigh* involves the pattern layer. The alphabet layer involves letter/sound relationships. The meaning layer involves the relationships between word meanings and their spellings. Conventional spelling refers to spelling words accurately.

35. C: Stage 1, Emergent Spelling: 3 to 5-year-olds begin writing letters without phonemic matches; they learn drawing/writing differentiation, letter formation, writing directionality, and some letter-sound associations. Stage 2, Letter Name-Alphabetic Spelling: 5 to 7-year-olds learn the alphabetic principle, consonant and short vowel sounds, consonant blends, and digraphs. Stage 3, Within-Word Pattern Spelling: 7 to 9-year-olds learn long vowel spelling patterns, r-controlled vowels, more complex consonant patterns, diphthongs, and other less-frequent vowel patterns. Stage 4, Syllables and Affixes Spelling: 9 to 11-year-olds learn inflectional endings and rules, syllabication, and homophones. Stage 5, Derivational Relations Spelling: 11 to 14-year-olds learn consonant and vowel alternations, Greek and Latin roots and affixes, and etymologies.

36. A: According to the National Research Council (Snow, Burns, and Griffin, 1998), phonological awareness is the general ability to distinguish speech sounds from their meanings, whereas phonemic awareness is a more specific ability to distinguish individual speech sounds, i.e., phonemes, within words. Hence phonemic awareness is the most sophisticated level of phonological awareness (D). Therefore, choice B and C are also incorrect.

Copyright © Mometrix Media. You have been licensed one copy of this document for personal use only. Any other reproduction or redistribution is strictly prohibited. All rights reserved.
This content is provided for test preparation purposes only and does not imply an endorsement by Mometrix of any particular political, scientific, or religious point of view.

37. C: Decoding monosyllabic words by referring to the initial and final consonant, short vowel, and long vowel sounds represented by their letters is a common academic standard for 1st-grade students. Typical academic standards for kindergarten students include demonstrating knowledge of letter-sound correspondences; understanding the alphabetic principle; matching letters to their corresponding consonant (and short vowel) sounds; and reading simple, monosyllabic sight words, i.e., high-frequency words.

38. B: Once children have learned the basic rules and principles for spelling in their native language, they can usually figure out how to spell words that are new to them when they hear them spoken. As children accrue experience in communicating with language, they notice basic patterns in letter combinations, syllables, common word roots, prefixes, suffixes, endings, etc., so much of their knowledge of spelling patterns comes through incidental learning (A). Also, children usually can read words that they can spell (C). Therefore, not only do their reading and writing skills support correct spelling, but reciprocally, good spelling skills also support children's reading and writing (D).

39. B: Research findings show that it helps ELL students for teachers to assign them in pairs, particularly for projects (a), experiments, and reports; to write problems and directions for them using shorter, simpler sentences (b); to emphasize student work accuracy much more than student work speed (c); and to ask ELL students many questions that they must use higher level cognitive processes to answer (d).

40. D: Teachers should give students learning English as a second language (ESL) and English language learners (ELLs) clear models and examples of what they expect them to do, how to do it, and how the completed results should look. Stating directions verbally in English alone is insufficient for students learning a foreign language. Teachers must also give ELLs more time to respond because it takes them longer to process the English they hear, mentally translate it into their own language, mentally formulate a response in their own language, translate that mentally into English, and judge whether their translation makes sense before they answer. It typically takes ESLs years before they can "think in English." When using idioms and figures of speech, teachers should explain these to ELLs and add pantomime demonstrations to help them understand. These expressions are not logical and often have no L1 equivalents for ESLs, so they require explicit instruction.

41. C: Oral language is a vital aspect of any language arts instruction. Often, the first concepts of language are transmitted via oral and auditory processes. The first Americans also possessed a rich oral culture in which stories and histories were passed down through generations via storytelling. Inviting a guest speaker who is part of this culture helps students understand more about cultures in their world, as well as the value of oral language and storytelling. This introduction gives students a relevant personal experience with which to connect what they will be learning in class.

42. B: In cases of words that sound alike but have different meanings, checking a dictionary or thesaurus will ensure correct usage of a word.

43. D: To instruct students in word analysis following a sequence progressing from simpler to more complex, teachers would first introduce individual phonemes (speech sounds); then the blending of two or more individual phonemes; then onsets and rimes (i.e., phonograms and word families) such as -*ack*, -*ide*, -*ay*, -*ight*, -*ine*, etc.; then the easier short vowels, followed by the more difficult long vowels; then blends of individual consonants; then CVC (consonant-vowel-consonant) words (e.g., *bag*, *hot*, *red*, *sit*) and other common patterns of consonants and vowels in words; and then the six most common types of syllables (i.e., closed, VCe, open, vowel team, *r*-controlled, and C-*le*).

Copyright © Mometrix Media. You have been licensed one copy of this document for personal use only. Any other reproduction or redistribution is strictly prohibited. All rights reserved.
This content is provided for test preparation purposes only and does not imply an endorsement by Mometrix of any particular political, scientific, or religious point of view.

44. B: Early Production, with the characteristics named, is the second stage of ESL acquisition. Preproduction (A), the first stage, involves no English speech, minimal listening comprehension, and the ability to draw pictures of and/or point at objects represented by some English words. Speech Emergence (C) is the third stage, characterized by good English comprehension; English speech using simple sentences, but still showing pronunciation and grammatical errors; and frequently misunderstanding English-language jokes. Intermediate Fluency (D), the fourth stage, features excellent English listening comprehension and few spoken grammatical errors.

45. C: The acronym *K.I.M.* in a K.I.M. vocabulary chart stands for Key idea, Information, and Memory clue. Under the "K" for Key idea, the student enters a vocabulary word. Under the "I" for Information, the student enters the definition of the word. Under the "M" for Memory clue, students often make a drawing or attach a picture, sometimes including written or printed captions, to remind them of the word's meaning.

46. A: Cooperative learning occurs when a group of students at various levels of reading ability have goals in common. Reading comprehension is achieved through reading both orally and silently, developing vocabulary, a reader's ability to predict what will occur in a piece of writing, a reader's ability to summarize the main points in a piece of writing, and a reader's ability to reflect on the text's meaning and connect that meaning to another text or personal experience.

47. B: Semantic maps are used to create visual representations of connections between items. Students can put the root in the middle of the semantic map and display words containing the root on the branches, thus demonstrating what the words have in common. Looking up words in the dictionary or finding them in the textbook does not facilitate making connections unless follow-up discussions or activities occur. While Venn diagrams are used to compare and contrast two or more things, the web-like format of the semantic map better displays the connections between related words.

48. C: Educational researchers (cf. Pardede, 2011) observe that novels can be too long for public school classes to read in limited time (A). Students typically require extensive instruction and time to understand figurative devices and other unfamiliar language in poems (B). Though students can be assigned to read drama, it is often impracticable for crowded classes with limited hours to act out a play (D). In contrast, short stories (C) can be read in one sitting and typically have one plot, fewer characters than novels, and brief, not detailed, setting descriptions, making it easier for students to follow a storyline.

49. A: Researchers find that student engagement can be deeper through integrating their practice with evaluating information sources into ongoing topic discussions; thus (B) is incorrect. Teachers should provide students with *short* passages excerpted from various resources related to the discussion topic (C). They can assign students to individual, paired, or small-group work evaluating material, which they should do using a *few, set* questions, not unlimited, open-ended ones (D), to guide their evaluations.

50. A: Word maps, which are ways to visually organize concepts, are good ways to introduce new vocabulary words and concepts to students in a classroom. Word maps provide a way for students to clearly detail a new vocabulary word and its definition, and also a way to create connections to both the word and the definition. This allows for the students to have a deeper understanding of the new concept, and to ideally form a connection with it so they can build permanent connections in their mind to the vocabulary word. Dictionaries, word walls, and using new vocabulary words regularly can all be helpful in the classroom, but for students to have the best chance to learn new

Copyright © Mometrix Media. You have been licensed one copy of this document for personal use only. Any other reproduction or redistribution is strictly prohibited. All rights reserved.
This content is provided for test preparation purposes only and does not imply an endorsement by Mometrix of any particular political, scientific, or religious point of view.

vocabulary, they need to have an opportunity to work with the word and form their own connections to it.

51. B: Concept mapping helps students to visualize, organize, and apply the concepts they have learned. Reading for meaning helps students read actively, including predicting, identifying main ideas/themes, inferring, analysis, comparison, evaluation, etc. Cloze procedures help students develop sequencing awareness and linguistic relationships; search, predict, and reconstruct; and determine meaning from context. Case studies help students apply content knowledge and skills through case analysis and explanation.

52. B: Inferring requires readers to use clues rather than explicit evidence to determine the author's meaning. Choice B requires students to use the character's statements to infer how he or she felt at the time. Choice A requires students to evaluate the writing. Choice C requires students to make a prediction. Choice D requires students to make a text-to-text connection.

53. D: Varying levels of explicit instruction, assigning small groups, and varying amounts of writing instruction time (A) reflects the principle of incorporating differentiated instruction. Allowing enough time for systematic writing opportunities in all content subjects as well as ELA classes (B) reflects the principle of integrating teaching writing across the curriculum. Incorporating reasons and methods for explicit writing instruction (C) reflects the principle of including rationales and methods of explicit writing instruction. Effective organization, spelling, vocabulary, syntax, etc., for different subjects (D) reflect the principle of teaching knowledge that enables more effective writing.

54. A: A KWL chart is a type of graphic organizer that teachers can have students make to assist them with reading comprehension. K stands for *know*: before reading, students record what they already know about the subject of a text. W stands for *want*: before and during reading, students record what they want to know about the subject. L stands for *learned*: after reading, students record what they learned from reading the text.

55. D: Analogies are used to help students recognize the relationships between words. Students are commonly given a pair of words whose relationship they must first identify. They then apply the same type of relationship to complete another word pair. Analogies can be used to help students recognize many different types of relationships, including recognizing synonyms, antonyms, and more. While students may explore word structure, definitions, and origins while completing analogies, the overall objective of analogies is to recognize and apply relationships between sets of words.

56. C: Picture walks are frequently used to activate students' prior knowledge. When readers look at the pictures, they make connections between the content of the new texts and what they already know from other texts or life experiences. These connections can spark interest in the stories and deepen comprehension. Teachers may encourage the use of syntactic cues during guided reading groups, but this is not typically part of a picture walk. Setting a purpose for reading is another beneficial prereading activity, but it is not always a part of a picture walk either. Metacognitive skills, which assist students with self-monitoring during reading, are also beneficial, but they are not typically the focus of a picture walk.

57. D: To allow Joshua more time and energy to focus on his essay, he can record only key words and phrases in his notes rather than writing complete sentences. This will also make it easier for him to locate the key information in his notes when he is ready to add it to his essay. Grouping notes into categories and using visuals can be beneficial, but based on Joshua's notes, recording the

Copyright © Mometrix Media. You have been licensed one copy of this document for personal use only. Any other reproduction or redistribution is strictly prohibited. All rights reserved.
This content is provided for test preparation purposes only and does not imply an endorsement by Mometrix of any particular political, scientific, or religious point of view.

key words and phrases is the most pressing need. Recording only a few facts may not provide enough information to complete an entire three-paragraph essay, so it would be more helpful to record additional facts in a more concise manner.

58. D: Literal comprehension is what text states overtly, e.g., story characters, event sequences, stated facts, etc. Choices A and B are examples of literal comprehension responses. Inferential comprehension is deeper or implicit meaning not explicitly stated, which readers must infer by considering text and drawing conclusions, e.g., unstated main ideas, cause-and-effect relationships, generalizations, and predictions. Choice C is an example of an inferential comprehension response. Evaluative comprehension requires readers to form opinions after analyzing text information. Choice D is an example of an evaluative comprehension response.

59. D: For written composition, teachers should instruct students to consider not only who their expected audience is, but also the format in which the audience will read or hear their work (A), which will inform how they write. Who the audience is affects the reading level(s), vocabulary, length, and type of writing the audience expects (D). It also affects what message each student wants to convey (B) just as much as the format does (C). They should not consider any one of these above any other, but consider all equally.

60. A: Choice A includes the current student performance level, the desired student performance level, the assessment used to determine the performance level, and the date the goal is expected to be achieved. Choice B only indicates the desired performance level and the assessment that will be used. Choice C indicates the assessment that will be used and the date the goal is expected to be achieved, but saying that it "will increase his oral reading rate" is too vague. It does not list the current or desired performance levels. Choice D only indicates the expected performance level and the assessment that will be used. It does not indicate the current performance level or the date the goal is expected to be achieved.

61. C: When a student has trouble recognizing words out of context (A), this is mainly a sign that the student has problems with decoding words, as is slow, laborious oral reading one word at a time (B). Having trouble differentiating main ideas or important information from minor details (C) in text is mainly a sign that the student has problems with reading comprehension. Having trouble relating text to his or her own existing knowledge (D) is mainly a sign that the student has problems retaining reading information.

62. C: Practical instructional activities that develop student listening skills (cf. Wolvin and Coakley, 1979) include teaching students both to follow (A) and give (B) directions, teaching them interpersonal communication skills (C), and teaching them to appreciate oral literature (D).

63. A: In shared writing experiences, students share thoughts during a class discussion, and the teacher records them on paper. Because students are in the preliterate stage of writing, they are not yet using sound/symbol relationships to spell words. Writing at this stage may resemble scribbling or contain strings of pretend letters. If Mr. Suarez records the students' thoughts for this activity, the story can be reread multiple times. If students write independently or with partners, it will be difficult to maintain the message of the story each time it is reread. Similar difficulties would occur with interactive writing because students help write the shared story on paper.

64. A: Evaluative questions require readers to form opinions or judgements based on the text. Asking if readers agree with something the author stated is an evaluative question. The remaining questions ask students to recall information only.

Copyright © Mometrix Media. You have been licensed one copy of this document for personal use only. Any other reproduction or redistribution is strictly prohibited. All rights reserved.
This content is provided for test preparation purposes only and does not imply an endorsement by Mometrix of any particular political, scientific, or religious point of view.

65. B: Schemata are units of existing knowledge used to make sense of newly encountered information. Readers rely on their existing schemata to make sense of information encountered in new texts. Therefore, activating prior knowledge is a key component of schema theory. For example, a child may know that flowers require water to grow. He may use this existing schema to make sense of a new text about the desert, which indicates that few plants grow there. Summarizing, identifying main idea, and recognizing story elements all require finding key information within a text, but they do not necessarily relate this information to what was already known about the topic prior to reading.

66. A: I-Charts or Inquiry Charts guide students to collect evidence from multiple information sources to support their ideas. While I-Charts are one type of graphic organizer, graphic organizers in general (B) organize and depict information more visually and simply; many do not involve finding or organizing information sources as I-Charts do. Journaling (C) helps students develop their own ideas rather than find or use evidence to support them. RAFT (D), i.e., Reader, Audience, Format, Topic, is a reading or writing strategy that helps students understand those four components' roles, comprehend informational text, and think creatively rather than find and use supporting evidence.

67. C: William is making errors in subject-verb agreement. Singular nouns should be paired with singular verbs, and plural nouns should be paired with plural verbs. Pronoun-antecedent agreement refers to ensuring that pronouns agree with their antecedents in number and gender. The sentences in this example do not include pronouns. There are no errors present in verb tense or sentence complexity. Verb consistency refers to ensuring that the verbs within a piece of writing use the same tense. Complex sentences are sentences that contain at least one dependent and independent clause.

68. D: Denotative meanings are the literal meanings of words found when they are looked up in the dictionary. Connotative meanings are the ideas or feelings evoked by the words. Therefore, two words can have the same denotative meaning in the dictionary, yet evoke very different reactions from readers. *Frugal* and *cheap* can both mean costing little, yet *cheap* often carries a negative connotation. For example, people may be insulted if they were called cheap, yet take pride in being referred to as frugal. The remaining pairs of words have similar meanings, and they all evoke positive feelings.

69. A: A story map outlines the main elements of the story, including the characters, setting, conflict, plot, and resolution. Recording these elements will assist the student in remembering and analyzing the story after it has been read. If the student has retention issues, he or she may not recall the story elements even after reading the story twice or listening to an audio version. A KWL chart can be used to activate prior knowledge and help the student reflect on what was learned, but it does not outline the story elements needed to analyze plot.

70. A: Among instructional strategies defined by a master teacher (Robb, 2002), asking students open-ended questions about the texts they read is most useful for helping students to read critically. Teaching students how to skim text for headings, subheadings, boldface, illustrations, captions, sidebars, the index, and other text features that give signs (B) of pertinent material is most useful for helping students locate information. Guiding students to make connections between text and their own personal experiences (D), everyday life (C), world events, and other texts is most useful for helping students understand the relevance of learning materials.

71. D: Although some history textbooks may use narrative (A) writing to make historical events more interesting by telling a story, these are not in the majority. Persuasive (B) writing seeks to

Copyright © Mometrix Media. You have been licensed one copy of this document for personal use only. Any other reproduction or redistribution is strictly prohibited. All rights reserved. This content is provided for test preparation purposes only and does not imply an endorsement by Mometrix of any particular political, scientific, or religious point of view.

convince readers to agree with the author's position; most content-area textbooks used in public schools present information more objectively. Descriptive (C) writing seeks to convey a vivid impression of something by providing sensory details so readers feel they are experiencing it; most content-area textbooks are more factual. The majority of school content textbooks use informational (D) writing to impart knowledge.

72. B: Indirect ways in which students receive instruction and learn vocabulary include through daily conversations, reading on their own, and being read aloud to by adults. Direct instruction and learning in vocabulary include teachers providing extended instruction exposing students repeatedly to vocabulary words in multiple teaching contexts, teachers pre-teaching specific words found in text prior to students reading it, and teachers instructing students over extended time periods and having them actively work with vocabulary words.

73. B: Analogies are easier for children to understand because they compare known items, whereas metaphors require abstract thinking.

74. A: Phonics instruction in the early grades has proved most beneficial in developing reading proficiency. Storytelling teaches important speaking and listening skills, but these are different from reading skills. While real literature may increase students' interest in reading, basal texts are well-designed to teach the essential skills.

75. B: The topics of cooperative projects and/or discussions and whether they are age-appropriate in difficulty relate most to cognitive developmental levels, i.e., what they can understand. Social developmental levels (a) relate to whether students can interact effectively in peer groups. Emotional developmental levels (c) relate to student emotional intelligence, i.e., emotional self-management plus sensitivity to, understanding of, and appropriate response to others' emotions. Behavioral developmental levels (d) relate to whether students can regulate their behaviors appropriately within peer groups.

76. B: English language learners (ELLs) generally benefit from contextual learning of vocabulary because it helps to solidify the meaning and usage of the newly-learned words. Both vocabulary in isolation (a) and vocabulary in volume (b) typically refer to rote memorization, which does not provide the retention benefits or provide the student with contextual experience. Answer (d) is wrong because speech proficiency levels do not necessarily correspond to a student's reading and vocabulary skills.

77. D: Having classmates offer peer reviews (a), having the teacher evaluate their work (b), and comparing their work to that of their classmates (c) are all valuable sources of feedback for students about their performance and progress in speaking and enacting through oral reports and presentations as they give different perspectives; however, video recordings of student performance (d) are the only type of completely objective feedback among these choices because they provide an exact record of what the student did. This enables students to self-monitor, make changes/improvements, and appreciate their own progress over time.

78. B: In this paired reading strategy, which improves reading comprehension and helps students identify the main idea in informational text, after silently reading a text selection, the pair of students takes turns following these steps: One student paraphrases what he or she thinks the text's main idea is. The other student agrees or disagrees, explaining why. The pair then develops a consensus as to the text's main idea. Then they take turns finding details in the text that support its main idea.

Copyright © Mometrix Media. You have been licensed one copy of this document for personal use only. Any other reproduction or redistribution is strictly prohibited. All rights reserved.
This content is provided for test preparation purposes only and does not imply an endorsement by Mometrix of any particular political, scientific, or religious point of view.

79. D: Making at least the attempt to read every single word, even with many errors (A), is a strategic strength that gives students decoding practice and, even without success every time, enables their potential. Attending to punctuation in text (B) is a strength, since punctuation can significantly affect meaning (e.g., "Let's eat, Grandma" vs. "Let's eat Grandma"). Even without understanding all details, getting the gist of text meaning (C) is also a strength. However, holistic word reading (D) misses plural or verb tense endings and other morphological changes affecting meaning, reflecting a strategic weakness.

80. C: Bias occurs when a test disadvantages a certain group of students. Including questions with cultural references that only a select group of students will understand disadvantages other students who do not understand the references. Students may miss these questions, despite having the reading skills the test is supposed to measure. Validity refers to whether the test measures what it is supposed to measure. Reliability relates to consistency of the test results over time and between participants.

81. B: Performance-based assessments do not involve comparing student performance to norms (A) as standardized tests do. Rather, they evaluate each student's (in this case, literacy) skills based on how that student performs or by products he or she produces. Thus, teachers must establish clear, equitable criteria (B) for evaluating these, because there will not be a single correct answer (C). Student responses will vary widely, so teachers must use these criteria plus their own judgment, not standardized answer keys (D).

82. C: Being able to repeat English words and phrases (A) and name concrete objects on sight (B) are both examples of criteria at the lowest level of an oral ELP scoring rubric. Being able to communicate well in social contexts (D) is an example of a rubric criterion for an intermediate ELP level. At the highest level, the student would communicate *very* well, not only in social but also academic contexts. Being able to participate in classroom discussions (C) is an example of the highest ELP level.

83. A: The *first* thing the teacher should do is always to ask the child if he or she knows what rhyming words are. If the child answers yes, the teacher should ask the child to say two rhyming words (B). If the child gives an incorrect example, or has answered no to the question, the teacher should then explain to the child the definition of rhymes (C). After explaining, the teacher should then give the child an example of two rhyming words (D). The teacher can then offer other word pairs and have the child identify whether they rhyme or not. Once the child masters this, the teacher can ask the child to say two rhyming words again.

84. B: In choice B, the student substituted the word *seven* for *several*, and read the rest of the sentence correctly. The words *seven* and *several* are visually similar, as the first four letters are the same in each. Choices A and D demonstrate errors related to meaning, as the student substituted words that made sense in the sentences but were not visually similar to the existing words. Choice D contains an omission, as the student did not say *several*.

85. C: Screening assessments are given to identify students who may be at future risk of academic difficulties and may benefit from interventions. Diagnostic assessments can then be given to confirm or provide additional information about screening results, including identifying students' specific strengths and needs. This information can then be used to guide instruction.

86. A: Progress monitoring is a type of assessment used to track students' progress towards certain goals over time. When students are receiving reading interventions, frequent progress monitoring should be done to assess their progress and determine if the interventions are succeeding.

Copyright © Mometrix Media. You have been licensed one copy of this document for personal use only. Any other reproduction or redistribution is strictly prohibited. All rights reserved. This content is provided for test preparation purposes only and does not imply an endorsement by Mometrix of any particular political, scientific, or religious point of view.

Screening is done initially to determine if students are at risk for academic difficulties, and it is done at greater intervals, such as the start of each school year. Summative assessment occurs at the end of a unit of study or other larger unit of instruction. Norm-referenced tests compare students' performances to the performances of sample groups of similar students, while progress monitoring is done to assess students' progress towards their own personal goals.

87. D: In choice D, the student read the sentence correctly, except for changing *chases* to *chased*. *Chased* still sounds right in the sentence, indicating that the student was using structural, or syntactic, cues to decode the word. In choice A, the student replaced *stick* with *branch*. *Branch* makes sense in the sentence, and it is not visually similar to the existing word. Choice B demonstrates an insertion, as the student added the word *big*. Choice C demonstrates a visual error, as the student replaced *furry* with *fuzzy*. Both words are visually similar.

88. B: Advanced readers and writers should be given opportunities to explore concepts using high-level thinking skills. If they have already mastered identifying adjectives, then evaluating adjective choices in a text and selecting stronger options would be a more challenging activity. Proficient readers and writers should not simply be given additional amounts of unchallenging work, as suggested in options A and D. Pairing students with differing skill levels can have instructional benefits, but the activities should be structured to ensure that both students benefit from the interactions.

89. C: In choice C, students listen and watch as their teacher reads a print-based book aloud, and then they use a digital tool to create a multimedia presentation. This combines both digital and print-based media. Choice A consists of two print-based activities. Choices B and D each contain two digital activities.

90. D: Studies have found some CAI not only increases literacy skills, but also attention and interaction in students with disabilities that include autism, cerebral palsy, Down syndrome, and intellectual disability (A). Using multimedia software (e.g., Delta Messages) plus instructional scaffolding is found effective for students not performing well with conventional instruction (B). Combining CAI with the Nonverbal Reading Approach for students with co-existing severe speech disorders and physical disabilities or autism was found effective, but not necessarily more effective than teacher-only instruction or teacher-plus-CAI (C). Acquisition rates depended on individual students, showing the importance of individualizing instruction (D) for this population.

91. A: The child will feel more confident because the story is already familiar, so this strategy is useful. She will also feel that the lesson is a conversation of sorts, and that she is communicating successfully. She will be motivated to learn the English words because they are meaningful and highly charged. As a newly arrived immigrant, the child feels overwhelmed. Presenting her with a book of folk tales from her country tells her that she needn't lose her culture in order to function in this one. It also comforts her by reminding her that her past and present are linked. Allowing her to speak in Korean helps her express herself without fear of judgment or failure. Presenting her with an English vocabulary that is meaningful ensures that she will eagerly embrace these words, her first words in her new language.

92. C: One of the challenges of large-group instruction is meeting the needs of diverse learners. Reading a novel aloud helps to make the content accessible to all learners. If students were to read it independently, as in choice B, the text would likely not be challenging enough for some readers and too difficult for others. Therefore, basing a comprehension lesson on a book that was read

Copyright © Mometrix Media. You have been licensed one copy of this document for personal use only. Any other reproduction or redistribution is strictly prohibited. All rights reserved. This content is provided for test preparation purposes only and does not imply an endorsement by Mometrix of any particular political, scientific, or religious point of view.

aloud assists all students with participating. While teachers sometimes introduce and practice phonics skills in large groups, students are likely to have differing skill levels in this area. Proficient first-grade readers, for example, may read consonant blends and digraphs with ease, which struggling readers may still be learning the alphabetic principle. Students in a classroom are also likely to have vastly different spelling skills, making the need for differentiation important.

93. D: Researchers have found that explicit instruction in phonics does help students at risk for reading failure particularly, but also promotes higher achievement by all students (A). Research supports the use of decodable books (B) early in first grade. Studies find that the kind of text read by students affects the word identification strategies they use (C), and also that prior student literacy knowledge (indicated by reading readiness assessment), as well as using decodable texts early, contribute to developing understanding of sound-spelling relationships (D).

94. B: While school and classroom computers are increasingly common, many districts and schools still struggle with underfunding and insufficient or inadequate technological equipment (or personnel). One solution is using smartphones, which some teachers project will become the most inexpensive teaching tool (A) for one-to-one connectivity and computing due to their popularity, ubiquity, mobility, and portability. While they have secured corporate sponsors to donate phones for students needing them, these teachers advise letting students who have them use their own phones (B). They also advise creating an acceptable use policy (C) and finding good ways of getting information from students' phones (D).

95. B: Designing a K-12 reading curriculum requires systematic planning, but NOT following a series of steps in rigid order (A). Design pursues optimal functionality, not perfection; despite all efforts to plan systematically and think inventively, compromises among everyone's wishes are inevitable (B). Decisions made at different stages are NOT independent, but interact (C); hence, the design process is often recursive. Though educators may revisit different stages, to make the design process work, they must recognize each stage's challenges and tasks. The first stage is setting design specifications; stages of conceptualizing, developing, and refining the design follow (D).

96. B: LEAD21 (Wright Group, McGraw-Hill) identifies four central components of reading instruction: (1) teachers read to students, (2) teachers read with large student groups, (3) teachers read with small student groups, and (4) individual students read. Choice A represents four sizes of grouping in reading instruction. Choice C represents four types of instructional activities for reading. Choice D represents four types of grouping in reading instruction.

97. C: In LEAD21 (Wright Group, McGraw-Hill) reading instruction, teacher expectations, and student tasks (A) are kept uniform across all students, while the choices of texts and the levels of teacher support (B) are differentiated. Hence, choice C includes one factor that is not differentiated followed by one that is, while choice D includes one factor that is differentiated followed by one that is not.

98. C: Summative assessments are administered after instruction and less often than formative assessments, which teachers make more frequently during instruction (a) to inform changes to make their teaching more effective (b). Typical times for summative assessments are after each lesson, unit, and school year is completed (c). Teachers rely on formative, not summative assessments for individual student data (d); they rely on summative assessment results for group data and group comparisons.

99. A: Formative assessments are most often criterion-referenced tests, which measure a student's performance against a predetermined criterion that indicates success or proficiency. They are

Copyright © Mometrix Media. You have been licensed one copy of this document for personal use only. Any other reproduction or redistribution is strictly prohibited. All rights reserved. This content is provided for test preparation purposes only and does not imply an endorsement by Mometrix of any particular political, scientific, or religious point of view.

typically not norm-referenced tests (b), which measure a student's performance against the average performance (scores) of normative sample student groups, such as standardized tests used as summative assessments. Formative assessments may occasionally be standardized, but most frequently they are informal measures (c). They are not the most objective (d)—formal tests are— but formative assessments are better for monitoring student progress, evaluating teacher effectiveness, and informing instructional adjustments.

100. A: Teachers should generally use a variety of formal and informal assessment instruments to get a complete picture of student achievement. This is especially applicable for grouping students, which teachers should never do for the long term based on the results of only one assessment instrument. To conduct formative assessments of learning in progress, teachers should use both formal and informal test instruments; and use several different kinds, rather than choosing only one formal instrument to use exclusively. Formative assessment results are valuable not only for evaluating student progress, but moreover for use in the classroom as teaching tools.

Copyright © Mometrix Media. You have been licensed one copy of this document for personal use only. Any other reproduction or redistribution is strictly prohibited. All rights reserved. This content is provided for test preparation purposes only and does not imply an endorsement by Mometrix of any particular political, scientific, or religious point of view.